LANGUAGE IN USE

A PRE-INTERMEDIATE COURSE

SELF-STUDY
WORKBOOK
B

WITH ANSWER KEY

Adrian Doff
Christopher Jones

Cambridge University Press
Cambridge
New York   Port Chester   Melbourne   Sydney

Published by the Press Syndicate of the University of Cambridge
The Pitt Building, Trumpington Street, Cambridge CB2 1RP
40 West 20th Street, New York, NY 10011–4211, USA
10 Stamford Road, Oakleigh, Victoria 3166, Australia

© Cambridge University Press 1991

First published 1991
Split editions first published 1992

Printed in Great Britain by the Bath Press, Avon

ISBN 0 521 40602 1   Self-study Workbook with Answer Key
ISBN 0 521 37852 4   Self-study Workbook
ISBN 0 521 37851 6   Classroom Book
ISBN 0 521 37853 2   Teacher's Book
ISBN 0 521 37248 8   Class Cassette Set
ISBN 0 521 37247 X   Self-study Cassette Set

Split editions:
ISBN 0 521 40837 7   Self-study Workbook A with Answer Key
ISBN 0 521 40838 5   Self-study Workbook B with Answer Key
ISBN 0 521 40839 3   Self-study Cassette A
ISBN 0 521 40840 7   Self-study Cassette B
ISBN 0 521 40835 0   Classroom Book A
ISBN 0 521 40836 9   Classroom Book B

The right of the University of Cambridge to print and sell all manner of books was granted by Henry VIII in 1534. The University has printed and published continuously since 1584.

Acknowledgements

The authors and publishers would like to thank the following institutions and teachers for their help in testing the material and for the invaluable feedback which they provided.

ILI, Heliopolis, Egypt; The British Council, Cairo, Egypt; Lille University, Lille, France; IFG Langues, Paris, France; British Intstitute in Paris, Paris, France; IFERP, Paris, France; Beatrice Schildknecht, Wedel/Holstein, Germany; Heather Weyh, KONE, Hannover, Germany; The British Council, Athens, Greece; ELTE Radnóti Miklós Gyakorló Iskola, Budapest, Hungary; International House, Budapest, Hungary; Associazione Culturale delle Lingue Europee, Bologna, Italy; Teach In Language and Training Workshop, Rome, Italy; Cambridge Centre of English, Modena, Italy; British Institute of Florence, Florence, Italy; Toyohashi University of Technology, Toyohashi, Aichi-Ken, Japan; Cambridge School, Granollers, Spain; Senior Citizen Language and Cultural Centre, Zurich, Switzerland; Klubschule, Lichtensteig, Switzerland; Marmara Üniversitesi, Istanbul, Turkey; Yapi ve Kredi Bankasi, A.S., Istanbul, Turkey; Eyüboğlu Lisesi, Istanbul, Turkey; Ortadoğu Ingilizce Kurslari, Ankara, Turkey; London Study Centre, London, UK; Davies's School of English, London, UK; Eurocentre, Cambridge, UK; Studio School of English, Cambridge, UK; Newcastle College of Further Education, Newcastle, UK; Anglo World, Oxford, UK; International House, London, UK; Godmer House School of English, Oxford, UK; Chichester School of English, Chichester, UK.

The authors and publishers are grateful to the following copyright owners for permission to reproduce copyright material. Every endeavour has been made to contact copyright owners and apologies are expressed for any omissions.

p. 21: Illustrations and adapted text from the *Longman Illustrated Animal Encyclopedia*, edited by Dr Philip Whitfield, published 1984. Reprinted by kind permission of Longman Group UK.
p. 65: Reproduced and adapted from *The Usborne Book of Space Facts* by permission of Usborne Publishing Ltd, London.

The authors and publishers are grateful to the following illustrators:

Rowan Barnes-Murphy: pp. 41, 43, 59, 65, 76, 97, 107;
Helena Greene: pp. 13,32;
Lisa Hall: pp. 11*t*, 69;
Jeremy Long: pp. 11*b*, 12, 39, 44, 66;
Michael Ogden: pp. 30, 48;
Bill Piggins: pp. 17, 18, 36, 50, 51, 56, 63, 74, 81, 82, 108;
Sue Shields: p. 93;
Tess Stone: pp. 20, 99;
Kathy Ward: p. 94;
Annabel Wright: pp. 23, 24, 28, 29, 47, 70, 92;
Clare Wyatt: pp. 52, 88, 91.

t = top   *b* = bottom

Contents

To the student

This Workbook contains exercises for you to do on your own.

Each Workbook unit begins with grammar or vocabulary exercises, which give extra practice in the language you have learned in class.

In addition, there are self-study exercises which help you to develop particular skills in English. These are:
- Listening skills (in each unit)
- Reading skills (in each Grammar unit)
- Writing skills (in each Topic unit)
- Pronunciation (in Grammar units) and Sound and spelling (in Topic units)

There are also two Self-study Cassettes that go with the Workbook. You will need to use these for the Listening, Pronunciation, Sound and spelling, and Dictation exercises.

Answers to most of the exercises are given in the Answer key at the back of the book.

Here is a short description of the exercises in the Workbook:

Grammar exercises
The grammar exercises give practice in the main structures of the unit. They usually include one puzzle or word game, and sometimes one freer exercise. There are three or four grammar exercises in each unit.

Translation
This section contains sentences for you to translate into your own language – and then back into English.

🔲 Listening
These are short listening tasks, which give you a chance to listen to natural English in your own time. Usually, the speakers are doing one of the activities from the Classroom Book.

🔲 Pronunciation
These exercises give practice in pronunciation, stress and intonation.

🔲 Dictation
You hear a short text taken from one of the Classroom Book exercises, and write it down.

Reading
This section contains reading tasks based on a variety of short texts. These include magazine and newspaper articles, personal letters, jokes, quizzes and stories.

Vocabulary exercises
The vocabulary exercises give practice in the main vocabulary areas of the unit. They usually include one puzzle or word game, and sometimes one freer exercise. There are two or three vocabulary exercises in each unit.

New words
This is a space for you to write down new words from the unit, together with your own notes and examples.

Translation
This section contains sentences for you to translate into your own language – and then back into English.

Listening
These are short listening tasks, which give you a chance to listen to natural English in your own time. Usually, the speakers are doing one of the activities from the Classroom Book.

Sound and spelling
This section deals with the relationship between sound and spelling in English.

Dictation
You hear a short text taken from one of the Classroom Book exercises, and write it down.

Writing skills
These exercises teach the basic writing skills you need to write a paragraph in English. These include punctuation, using pronouns, joining sentences and organising ideas.

Guide to units

Self-study Workbook	Classroom Book
13 Comparison	
Grammar exercises Listening: *The most and the least* Pronunciation: *Reduced vowels (3)* Reading: *Four planets*	Making comparisons; expressing preferences;describing outstanding features Grammar: comparative adjectives; than; superlative adjectives
14 About town	
Vocabulary exercises Listening: *Living in London* Sound and spelling: *Words with* y Writing skills: *Reason and contrast*	Vocabulary: amenities; giving directions; describing towns in general Reading and listening activity: *Los Angeles*
15 Past and present	
Grammar exercises Listening: *Have you ever ... ?* Pronunciation: *Falling intonation* Reading: *Varieties of English*	Talking about changes; announcing news; talking about experiences Grammar: Present perfect tense; still; not ... yet; Have you ever ... ?
16 Free time	
Vocabulary exercises Listening: *Rock climbing* Sound and spelling: *Words with* r Writing skills: *Sequence (2)*	Vocabulary: leisure activities; sports; likes and dislikes Reading and listening activity: *Board games round the world*
17 Obligation	
Grammar exercises Listening: *Radio phone-in* Pronunciation: *Rising intonation* Reading: *Rules of the game*	Giving rules; talking about obligation; giving advice Grammar: must(n't); (don't) have to; can('t); should(n't); ought (not) to
18 A day's work	
Vocabulary exercises Listening: *A security guard* Sound and spelling: *Hard and soft* c *and* g Writing skills: *Letter writing*	Vocabulary: names of jobs; talking about work; careers Reading and listening activity: *Applying for a job*
Revision and extension Units 13–18	

Self-study Workbook	Classroom Book
19 Narration	
Grammar exercises Listening: *Two stories* Pronunciation: *Intonation: questions* Reading: *Bad luck*	Talking about past events and their circumstances; telling stories **Grammar:** Past continuous tense; Past simple tense; when & while
20 People	
Vocabulary exercises Listening: *Famous people* Sound and spelling: *Long and short vowels* Writing skills: *Relative clauses (1)*	**Vocabulary:** physical appearance; age; personal characteristics **Reading and listening activity:** *The Dream Game*
21 Prediction	
Grammar exercises Listening: *Driving test* Pronunciation: *Contrastive stress* Reading: *Star gazing*	Making predictions; talking about consequences **Grammar:** will, won't & might; if/unless + Present simple; going to
22 Around the world	
Vocabulary exercises Listening: *Living in a hot climate* Sound and spelling: *Words with* s Writing skills: *Relative clauses (2)*	**Vocabulary:** geographical features; weather and climate; countries and nationalities **Reading and listening activity:** *Car chaos*
23 Duration	
Grammar exercises Listening: *24 hours* Pronunciation: *Dialogues* Reading: *General knowledge quiz*	Talking about activities that are still going on; asking and talking about duration **Grammar:** Present perfect continuous and simple; How long ...?; for & since; spend (+ -ing)
24 But is it art?	
Vocabulary exercises Listening: *Choosing a painting* Sound and spelling: *Words with* th Writing skills: *Sequence (3)*	**Vocabulary:** art and literature; writers, artists and performers **Reading and listening activity:** *The Night in the Hotel*
Revision and extension Units 19–24	

13 Comparison

A Comparative and superlative

Complete the table with comparative and superlative forms.

Adjective	Comparative	Superlative
clean	*cleaner*	*cleanest*
small		
fat		
wide		
heavy		
careful		
exciting		
intelligent		
good		
bad		
far		
much/many		

Comparative and superlative forms

One-syllable adjectives:
   cold – **colder** – **coldest**
   big – **bigger** – **biggest**

Two-syllable adjectives:
   ending in **y**:
   friendly – **friendlier** – **friendliest**
   most others:
   boring – **more boring** – **most boring**
   helpful – **more helpful** – **most helpful**

Three or more syllables:
   popular – **more popular** – **most popular**
   interesting – **more interesting** – **most interesting**

Irregular adjectives:
   good, bad, far, much/many

B Opposites

Rewrite each sentence using an opposite adjective.
The *first letters* of the adjectives in numbers 1–6 give the missing word in 7.

Example:

Geckos are *smaller* than crocodiles → Crocodiles *are bigger than geckos.*

1 Gold is *more expensive* than silver.

   Silver ....

2 Lambs are *younger* than sheep.

   Sheep ....

3 Steel is *heavier* than aluminium.

   Aluminium ....

4 California is *wetter* than Arizona.

   Arizona ....

5 Listening is *more difficult* than reading.

   Reading ....

6 The Third World is *poorer* than the West.

   The West ....

7 Mars is ☐ ☐ ☐ ☐ ☐ than Venus.

C World records

What world records can you find in the box? Some words are used more than once; some are not used.

Examples:

The Vatican is the smallest country in the world.
China has got the largest population in the world.

The Vatican	rich	population
China	high	caviare
The USSR	good	mountain
The whale	small	place
The cheetah	expensive	river
The Nile	sunny	fish
M.Everest	large	country
The Sahara	fast	mammal
Beluga	long	animal

1 ....

2 ....

3 ....

4 ....

5 ....

6 ....

7 ....

D People

Who's the most boring person you know?
Why is he/she boring?
Write about four people you know.

Example:

The most boring person I know is my younger brother. He just watches television all the time.

1 boring

....

....

....

2 intelligent

....

....

....

3 interesting

....

....

....

4 unusual

....

....

....

TRANSLATION

Translate into your own language:

1 I think she's the most intelligent
person I've ever met.

....
....

2 – What's the best way to get there?
  – Well, the bus is cheaper, but it's
  more comfortable by train.

....
....
....

3 – This is a good restaurant, isn't it?
  – I prefer Bruno's myself. I think the
  food's much better there.

....
....
....

Now cover up the left-hand side, and translate your sentences back into English.

LISTENING: The most and the least

You will hear three people (A, B, C) talking about
the musical instruments they play, the languages they
speak, and the countries they have visited.

1 Which person:

a is the most musical?   ....

b is the least musical?   ....

c speaks the most languages?   ....

d speaks the fewest languages?   ....

e has visited the most countries? ....

f has visited the fewest countries? ....

2 Listen again and answer these
questions.

a Which of the people still play(s)
the piano?   ....

b Which of the people could make
themselves understood in:
  – Switzerland?   ....
  – Mexico?   ....
  – Japan?   ....

c Which speakers do you think
have been to:
  – Switzerland?   ....
  – Mexico?   ....
  – Japan?   ....

PRONUNCIATION:
Reduced vowels (3)

1 Listen to the words in the box. They have a
full sound when they are stressed, but have
the sound /ə/ when they are unstressed.

are	Are you there?
	What are you doing?
can	Can you swim? Yes, I can.
	I think I can see them.
was	He wasn't at home. No,
	but I was.
	There was plenty of food.

2 Listen to these sentences. Is the word
pronounced (1) with a full sound?
(2) with the sound /ə/? Write 1 or 2.

a does ....   g does ....

b are ....   h were ....

c was ....   i was ....

d do ....   j are ....

e does ....   k were ....

f can ....   l was ....

Now listen again, and practise saying
the sentences.

DICTATION

You will hear four of the texts from
Outstanding features (Classroom Book,
page 61). Listen and write down what you
hear.

READING: Four planets

What do you know about the Solar System?
Mark these statements T (True) or F (False).
Then check your answers in the text.

☐ 1 A year on Pluto is more than 100 years on Earth.

☐ 2 Mercury is the nearest planet to the Sun.

☐ 3 The biggest hurricane in the Solar System is on Jupiter.

☐ 4 Mercury is the hottest planet.

☐ 5 Jupiter is bigger than all the other planets put together.

☐ 6 Mercury is heavier than Pluto.

☐ 7 The diameter of the Sun is more than 20 times bigger than the diameter of Jupiter.

☐ 8 Uranus is the furthest planet from Earth.

☐ 9 Earth's atmosphere is thinner than Venus's atmosphere.

☐ 10 Pluto is the smallest of the planets.

☐ 11 Venus is the easiest planet to see from Earth.

Mercury

Mercury is the closest planet to the Sun. Because of this, it has scorching daytime temperatures of up to 350°C. This is over seven times hotter than the hottest temperature ever recorded on Earth: 57.7°C at Azizia, Libya, in 1922.

At night, the temperature can drop to −170°C because there is no atmosphere to trap the heat. This is more than seven times colder than the temperature inside the freezer compartment of a refrigerator.

Jupiter

Jupiter is the largest planet in our Solar System. It is more than 1,300 times bigger than Earth, and bigger than all the other planets put together. But it is still much smaller than the Sun: if the Sun was the size of a tennis ball 8 cm in diameter, Jupiter would be the size of a pea 0.85 cm in diameter.

There is a reddish patch on Jupiter, known as the Great Red Spot. This is the biggest hurricane in the Solar System, with swirling clouds about 38,500 km long by 11,000 km wide. It is as big as three Earths.

Venus

Seen from Earth, Venus is by far the brightest of the planets. It is often called the "evening star". Although Venus and Earth are about the same size, their atmospheres are completely different. Venus's atmosphere is so thick that at the planet's surface the pressure is 90 times that on Earth. This thick atmosphere traps the Sun's heat rather like a greenhouse, so that the temperature reaches about 500°C.

Pluto

Pluto was discovered in 1930. With a diameter of 2,400 km, it is smaller than our Moon, making it the smallest and lightest planet in the Solar System.

For most of the time, Pluto is the furthest planet from Earth (sometimes Neptune is the furthest). An aeroplane travelling at a speed of 1,000 kph would take about 670 years to travel from Earth to Pluto.

A person on Pluto would never live for one Pluto year. The Pluto year is the time it takes Pluto to travel once round the Sun – about 147 years.

Adapted from *The Usborne Book of Space Facts*

14 About town

A Guests

Here are some guests you're expecting over the next few months. Write down some things that you'll do with them.

Has lots of money ... loves good food ... gets up at 11.30 ... lazy ... a night person
Take him to an expensive restaurant for dinner.
....
....

Cultured ... not very active ... doesn't go out after dark
....
....

Like doing and watching sports ... enjoy watching films ... interested in animals
....
....

Love shopping ... enjoy taking photographs ... good dancers
....
....

B Giving directions

Complete the conversations using expressions from the box.

Example:

A Excuse me, can you tell me the way to the Post Office?

B *Yes. You go straight along this road. Go over the river, and then turn right at the cinema. You'll see it on the left.*

Turn	left / right	(at ...)
Go straight on		
Go	under / over / past	...
You'll see it / It's	on the	left. / right.

A Excuse me, how do I get to the university?

B ....
....

A Excuse me, can you tell me the way to the swimming pool?

B ....
....

A Excuse me, ...

B ....
....

C Describing towns

Continue these descriptions of towns.

Examples:

It's a rather dirty town ... *There's a lot of traffic, and the streets are full of litter.*

It's a good place for old people to live ... *It's got a pleasant climate, there isn't much traffic, and there are lots of parks.*

1 It's a good place for students ... .

....

....

2 It's a very beautiful town ... .

....

....

3 It's a really boring place to live ... .

....

....

4 It's a good place to live if you've got young children ... .

....

....

New words

Use this space to write down new words from the unit, with your own notes and examples.

....

....

....

....

....

....

....

....

....

....

....

....

....

TRANSLATION

Translate into your own language:

1 – Excuse me. Is there a department
   store anywhere near here?
   – Yes, there's one just along the road.

....

....

....

2 There's a very good sports centre
  with a swimming pool, tennis courts
  and a football pitch.

....

....

....

3 There aren't many places to go in the
  evenings.

....

....

Now cover up the left-hand side, and translate your sentences back into English.

LISTENING: Living in London

You will hear a man and a woman talking about living in London.

1 Listen and complete the table.
  Which things does the man talk about? Which does the woman talk about? (Write M or W.)
  Do they think these are good or bad points? (Write *Good* or *Bad*.)

		M/W	Good/Bad
a	going to work		
b	going out in the evening		
c	noise		
d	people's behaviour		
e	food shops		
f	the city's atmosphere		

2 What do they say about each topic in the table above?
  Write a brief comment for each one.

a *The underground's always crowded.*
....

b ....

c ....

d ....

e ....

f ....

SOUNDS AND SPELLING: Words with *y*

1 Listen to these words on the tape.
  Group A: /i/ city, slowly, happy, angry
  Group B: /aɪ/ my, cry, why, flying

2 How do you say these words? Mark them A or B. Then listen to the tape.

	dry		typist
	carry		hungry
	friendly		trying

3 Sometimes, *y* changes to *ie*. For example:
  try – tries – tried;   carry – carries – carried
  city – cities;   happy – happier
  but: play – plays – played;   boy – boys

  You will hear sentences containing forms of these words. Write down the words.

  a marry   *c* easy   *e* party
  b cry   *d* enjoy   *f* stay

4 You will hear four sentences. Cover this page, and write them down.

DICTATION

You will hear one of the texts from *Los Angeles* (Classroom Book, page 67).

Listen and write down what you hear.

WRITING SKILLS: Reason and contrast

1 Look at these examples.

It's a very beautiful old city, **so** it's always full of tourists in summer.

As
Because | it's a very beautiful old city, it's always full of tourists in summer.

It's a very beautiful town to look at, **but** there isn't much to do there.
Although it's a very beautiful town to look at, there isn't much to do there.

2 Fill the gaps with *so*, *as*, *because*, *but* or *although*.

a .... there aren't many good restaurants, there are plenty of cheap cafés.

b .... it's a large sea port, it has a cosmopolitan atmosphere and there always a lot going on.

c There's a large theatre, ... they don't perform very interesting plays .... I don't go there very often.

d The river's very polluted .... it's not a good idea to swim in it, ... there's a very good swimming pool.

3 Join these ideas using words from the box. Change the order of the ideas if you like.

and	so
but	although
as	because

a It's a small town.
It's easy to get to know people.
People are very friendly.

....
....

b There are factories all round the town.
The air's very polluted.
It's a very unhealthy place to live.

....
....
....

c It's a large industrial town.
It's quite ugly.
I like living there.
It has a very friendly atmosphere.

....
....
....

d It's only a small town.
It's very lively.
There's lots to do in the evenings.
It's by the sea.
It's very popular with tourists.

....
....
....

15 Past and present

A Irregular squares

All the answers are past participles. They are all irregular verbs.

1 ▶ She has .... school now. She's at college. (4)

1 ▼ I've .... my coat. I can't find it anywhere. (4)

2 ▼ Ah, there it is. It's OK – I've .... it! (5)

3 ▶ Have you ever .... in the Black Sea? (4)

1 ▼ I've never .... in a tent before. (5)

2 ▶ I've .... across the Atlantic but I've never sailed. (5)

3 ▼ We've ....! We're the champions! (3)

4 ▶ Oh dear. I've .... too much money this week. (5)

1 ▼ They've just .... a new video recorder. (6)

2 ▶ Have you .... your bike yet? I'd like to buy it. (4)

3 ▼ Hey – you haven't .... the washing up yet. (4)

4 ▶ Tony's not here. He's .... to a meeting. (4)

1 ▼ I've paid two bills and .... three letters. (7)

2 ▶ He's .... a lot taller recently (5)

3 ▼ She's not asleep – she's just .... up. (5)

4 ▶ I've .... two aspirin, but my head still hurts. (5)

5 ▶ Have you ever .... to Shanghai? (4)

B Not ... yet

What hasn't happened yet? Rewrite each sentence using a verb from the box with *not ... yet*.

Example:

They're still here.
They haven't gone yet.

arrive
come back
find
get up
give up
go
leave

1 She's still looking for a flat.

....

2 They're still out.

....

3 He's still in bed.

....

4 We still smoke.

....

5 They're still waiting for the bus.

....

6 I'm still studying at university.

....

C Personal news

Imagine that you've just done three of these things:
- bought something – changed jobs – been ill – been on holiday
- moved house – met someone – lost something – broken up with a boyfriend/girlfriend

Write your news as part of a letter.

Examples:

I've been ill in bed this week. I had the 'flu, and I had to stay in bed, but I'm better now.

I'm afraid I've lost Helen's address. I can't find it anywhere. I'll ask her sister when I see her.

1 ....
....
....

2 ....
....
....

3 ....
....
....

D Questions of experience

Here are some answers. What were the questions?
Write a question with *Have you ever...?* for each.

1 Q: *Have you ever flown in a helicopter?* ....

A: Only once. It was very frightening.

2 Q: ....

A: No, never. But most of my friends have.

3 Q: ....

A: Yes, I have. I had to go to hospital.

4 Q: ....

A: Yes, twice. And the weather was wonderful both times.

5 Q: ....

A: Yes, I have. But no one could understand me.

6 Q: ....

A: No, I haven't. It's much too expensive.

7 Q: ....

A: Yes, I have – when I was a small child.

8 Q: ....

A: Only once. It was really exciting.

TRANSLATION

Translate into your own language:

1 We've just had a baby. It was born at three o'clock this morning.

....

....

2 – What do you think of Budapest?
  – I don't know. I've never been there.

....

....

4 – Have you finished that book yet?
  – No. I've only just started it.

....

....

Now cover up the left-hand side, and translate your sentences back into English.

LISTENING: Have you ever...?

Five people answer questions about their experiences.

1 Listen and guess what the questions were.

1 Have you ever ....?

2 Have you ever ....?

3 Have you ever ....?

4 Have you ever ....?

5 Have you ever ....?

2 Listen again and complete the table.

	The speaker has/hasn't...	When was it?	Did he/she enjoy it?
1			
2			
3			
4			
5			

3 Which speaker mentions these things? What does he/she say about them?

a a square   ....

b a birthday   ....

c the stage   ....

d money   ....

e the Old Vic theatre ....

PRONUNCIATION:
Falling intonation

1 In most sentences, the voice falls on the main stress. Listen to the examples.

No.

Yes.

Good.

I'm John.

It's raining.

What's your name?

They've gone to the cinema.

2 Look at these sentences. How do you think they are said? Mark the main stress with an arrow like this ＼ :

a I live in London.
b We need more petrol.
c Give it to me.
d The matches are in the cupboard.
e What are they doing?
f We've just bought a new house.
g They're watching television.

Now listen to the tape. Then practise saying the sentences.

DICTATION

You will hear part of the text from *Headline news* (Classroom Book, page 69).

Listen and write down what you hear.

READING: Varieties of English

1 What kinds of writing are these texts? Which of them is

a a note? ....
b the blurb on a book cover? ....
c a job application letter? ....
d a newspaper article? ....
e a personal letter? ....
f part of a novel? ....

2 Which texts do these questions refer to? What are the answers?

a Has he finished decorating his house? ....
b Is the fire now under control? ....
c Is their relationship finished? ....
d How many novels has she written? ....
e What job is he applying for? ....
f Who's been abroad? Did he enjoy it? ....

❶ David came to stay at the weekend. He's just come back from a trip to Algeria, where he set up some computer equipment. Algiers, I think it was, but he was a bit vague about it. Anyway, he sounds as if he had a really good time there and

❷ Although my degree was in Russian studies, I have taught both English and History, and I have a post-graduate teaching diploma. I should add that I also ran my own small business for several years, so I know a considerable amount about Business English. I would

❸ John and Helen

There wasn't any paint left for the doors, so I've gone to buy some more – I'll be back around 6. I've taken the car – sorry! There's a pizza in the fridge for the children's supper – could you heat it up for them when they come in? Thanks.

Mike

❹ Margaret Kyle was born in New York in 1955, and wrote her first novel, *Wildfire*, in 1976, while she was still at college. Since then, she has published four more novels and two collections of short stories. She now lives in Los Angeles, where she teaches modern American literature at UCLA. Margaret Kyle is married, and has three children.

❺ Fires were still raging over large areas near Kavala in Northern Greece yesterday, as the Government brought in army units to help fight the blaze. So far the fire has destroyed about 8000 hectares of forest, and attempts to control it using fire-fighting aircraft have been unsuccessful. Nearly 500 people have fled their homes in the area and have found temporary accommodation in Kavala and other nearby towns. Police have warned travellers to avoid the area, as they expect the fire to continue for several days.

❻ "Look, Alison," he said, quietly. "Things change. People change – and we've changed too. At least, I have."

"Changed? You?" She laughed harshly. He turned away, avoiding her eye, and stared out of the window.

"It's no good," he said. "I've made up my mind. I'm not coming back."

16 Free time

A Two kinds of activities

Read about Alison's and Barbara's leisure activities, and fill the gaps.

Alison's very musical. She sings and plays the (1▶), and most evenings she goes (3▶) with her friends in the local disco. She likes eating in restaurants, but she also enjoys (4▶) her own meals. She can (2▶), and has made quite a few jumpers and scarves. Alison also (5▶) stamps, and she enjoys (6▶) detective stories.

Barbara goes (7▶) every morning in the park. She enjoys athletics, especially the high-(8▶). She is also a great (9▶) fan, and goes to watch her team play every weekend. She enjoys horse-(10▶), and often plays a round of (11▶) at her local club. Barbara is a good driver, and goes (12▶)-racing whenever she can. When she's at home, you'll usually find her out in the (13▶), watering the flowers or cutting the grass.

The main difference between Alison and Barbara is that Alison enjoys (A▼) activities, whereas Barbara enjoys (B▼) activities.

B Go, play and do

Fill the gaps below with a suitable form of *go, play* or *do.*

1 I don't .... tennis very well because I don't .... enough practice.

2 He doesn't .... a lot of running – he .... jogging about once a month.

3 My sister enjoys .... chess, but I don't think she's ever .... Scrabble.

4 – We're .... swimming. Do you want to come?

   – No thanks. I'm .... basketball in two hours. And I .... swimming yesterday.

5 I .... some gardening yesterday morning, and then in the afternoon we all .... sailing; and in the evening we sat at home and .... cards.

C Likes and dislikes

Talk about leisure activities that you like and don't like. Say why.

Examples:

I enjoy listening to music. It helps me to relax.
I don't like playing computer games. I think they're very boring. And I never win.

Like/enjoy + ing or noun		
	like	swimming.
I	don't like	(playing) golf.
	enjoy	(watching) TV.
	don't enjoy	eating out.

1 ....

....

2 ....

....

3 ....

....

4 ....

....

New words

Use this space to write down new words from the unit, with your own notes and examples.

....

....

....

....

....

....

....

....

....

....

....

....

....

TRANSLATION

Translate into your own language:

1 – Are you going to the football match?
  – No, I think I'll stay at home and watch it on television.

....

....

....

2 We don't do much reading these days. We're too busy working.

....

....

3 – How about a game of chess?
  – I'm afraid I don't know how to play.

....

....

4 I really enjoy playing the piano, but I'm not very good at it.

....

....

Now cover up the left-hand side, and translate your sentences back into English.

LISTENING: Rock climbing

You will hear a woman talking about rock climbing.

1 Listen to the first part. Which of these statements are the same as what she says? (Write ✔ or ✗).

☐ a Rock climbing is interesting because you have to solve problems all the time.

☐ b Rock climbing is very strenuous and it needs a lot of endurance.

☐ c Hill walking is more strenuous than rock climbing.

☐ d Climbing small rocks is surprisingly easy.

☐ e Even easy climbs can be surprisingly absorbing.

☐ f Rock climbing is very different from most other sports.

2 In the second part, the woman talks about the time she was most frightened. Listen and choose the picture that matches her description best.

3 Write two sentences that could go in the bubble.

SOUND AND SPELLING: Words with r

You have already looked at some words with r: e.g. car, her, first, shore, turn.

Here are some new groups.

1 Listen to these words on the tape.
  Group A: /eə/ stair, chair, wear, share
  Group B: /ɪə/ cheer, clear, appear, here
  Group C: /aɪə/ wire, tired, flier, higher
  Group D: /aʊə/ our, flour, shower
  Group E: /jʊə/ pure, curious, secure

2 How do you say these words? Mark them A, B, C, D or E. Then listen to the tape.

☐ flower	☐ during
☐ hear	☐ we're
☐ they're	☐ fire
☐ cure	☐ where
☐ hour	☐ near
☐ hair	☐ drier

3 You will hear four sentences. Cover this page, and write them down.

DICTATION

You will hear part of the recording from *Leisure activities* (Classroom Book, page 72).

Listen and write down what you hear.

WRITING SKILLS: Sequence (2)

1 The words in the box below are used for showing sequence.
Find them in the texts and underline them.

first
then
and
after (a few minutes)
(an hour) later

> First we drove for a few miles along the main road, and then we turned down a narrow lane. Half an hour later we came to an old farmhouse.

> We went into the football stadium and found our seats. After about ten minutes, the crowd started cheering and the two teams came onto the pitch. A few minutes later the match began.

2 Rewrite these sentences with correct punctuation.

a I first met him at a party in London ....

about a year later I saw him again ....

b She put the phone down after a few ....

seconds she picked it up again and ....

dialled a number ....

3 Fill the gaps with sequence expressions from the box.

a We bought a programme .... found our seats. .... the

curtains opened .... the play began.

b A man went into the house .... closed the door. .... he

came out again carrying a black box.

c .... I had a long, hot bath, ... I sat in bed

.... read a book. .... I fell asleep.

4 Put this story in the correct order. Use sequence expressions to join the ideas together.

Monica knew exactly what to do.
The taxi arrived.
Edward arrived home.
She packed a small suitcase.
She called a taxi.
Monica closed the door and posted her keys through the letter box.
She wrote a letter and put it on the table.
The letter said 'Goodbye, Edward. I've had enough.'

Monica knew exactly what to do. ....

....

....

....

....

....

....

....

....

....

....

....

....

....

17 Obligation

A Obligation structures

Fill the gaps with expressions from the box.

must have to	mustn't can't
don't have to	can

<table>
<tr><td colspan="2">Must(n't), (don't) have to, can('t)</td></tr>
<tr><td>You must go
You have to go</td><td>= Go!</td></tr>
<tr><td>You mustn't go
You can't go</td><td>= Don't go!</td></tr>
<tr><td>You don't have to go</td><td>= Don't go if you
don't want to.</td></tr>
<tr><td>You can go</td><td>= Go if you want to.</td></tr>
</table>

1 – What time do you .... be home?

– I've got a key. I .... stay out as late as I like.

2 It's a secret. You .... tell anyone.

3 You .... take one pill three times a day. And you .... drink any alcohol.

4 Oh no! Is that the time? I .... go!

5 I love Sundays. I .... get up and I .... go to work. I .... lie in bed until lunch time if I want.

6 – .... I have a bath, please?

– Yes, of course you .... But you .... use too much hot water.

B Childish questions

Imagine you're a child in these situations. Ask questions with *Can ...?* or *Do ... have to ...?*
Example:
Your parents want to watch the news, and you want to watch *Disneytime.*
Can we watch Disneytime? or *Do we have to watch the news?*

1 You don't want to go to the dentist's.

....

2 You want chips for lunch, not a salad.

....

3 It's time for your friend to go home now.

....

4 It's bedtime for you and your brother.

....

5 It's pouring with rain, and your mother tells you it's time to go to school.

....

C Flying rules

Here are some questions about flying from someone who has never been in a plane.
What information can you give? (If you're not sure, ask someone yourself.)

Do I have to wear
a seat belt all
the time?

Can I take any
hand baggage?

I suppose I have to
take food and
drink with me.

Can I smoke?

Do I have to stay
in my seat?

You have to wear a seat belt during take-off and landing, and during bad weather. At other times, you can take it off.

....

....

....

....

....

....

D Giving advice

Finish these sentences with some good advice. For each
one, take two ideas from the box, and add one of your own.
Use *ought (not) to* and *should(n't)*.

should + *infinitive* ought + to + *infinitive*		
You	should ought to	give it back.
You	shouldn't ought not to	keep it.

arrive late	drink alcohol	take exercise
be polite	eat fatty food	wear a seat belt
dress smartly	smoke	work hard

1 If you want to pass an interview, *you should dress smartly, and you shouldn't arrive late.*
   And you ought to ask some intelligent questions at the end.

2 If you want a healthy heart, ...

   ....

   ....

   ....

3 If you want to drive safely, ...

   ....

   ....

   ....

4 If you want to run a successful business, ...

   ....

   ....

   ....

TRANSLATION

Translate into your own language:

1 – My shoulder still hurts.
– You ought to see a doctor about it.

....

....

2 – Can we have guests in our rooms?
– Yes you can, but they have to be
out by midnight.

....

....

....

3 DO NOT LEAN OUT OF THE WINDOW

....

4 He doesn't have to pay income
tax – he doesn't earn enough.

....

....

Now cover up the left-hand side, and translate your sentences back into English.

LISTENING: Radio phone-in

You will hear part of a radio phone-in programme, in which two experts give advice to listeners.

1 Listen to Susan's problem. Find five differences between this text and what you hear.

Susan, who is a student, has a generally bad relationship with her husband, who has just got a new job. In the evenings he likes to go out to parties. She prefers to stay at home and read, but he won't stay with her.

a ....

b ....

c ....

d ....

e ....

2 Which of these solutions do the two experts suggest? (Write 1, 2 or – .)

a Try to talk to him.   ....

b Do what he wants.   ....

c Do what you want.   ....

d Try to compromise.   ....

e Go out with friends.   ....

f Go out with another man.   ....

g Get a divorce.   ....

3 Now mark the advice that you think is best.

PRONUNCIATION:
Rising intonation

1 In some sentences, the voice *rises* at the end. This pattern is most often used in Yes/No questions. Listen to the examples and try saying them.

Yes? ⤴
Are you there? ⤴
Is that you, John? ⤴
Is it raining? ⤴
Have you been to London? ⤴
Did you enjoy the film? ⤴

2 Do you think these sentences have *falling* or *rising* intonation? Mark them with ⤴ or ⤵ .

a Hello.

b Hello?

c Are you busy?

d My name's Peter.

e Do you drink coffee?

f Where are you going?

g He's a friend of mine.

h He's a friend of yours?

Now listen to the tape. Then practise saying the sentences.

DICTATION

You will hear most of one text from *Personal problems* (Classroom Book, page 78).

Listen and write down what you hear.

READING: Rules of the game

Which of these 'rules' for football, basketball and tennis are *true* and which are *false*?
Write T or F by each one, and then check your answers in the key.

Basketball

1 ☐ You can shoot at the basket from any part of the basketball court.

2 ☐ You mustn't run while holding the ball.

3 ☐ A game of basketball cannot result in a draw: one side must win.

4 ☐ You can stand holding the ball for as long as you like.

5 ☐ If you have committed five fouls in a single game, you must leave the game.

Football

6 ☐ For a goal to be scored, the ball must go right over the goal line, not just part of the way.

7 ☐ You mustn't deliberately touch the ball with your arm.

8 ☐ The goalkeeper mustn't leave the goal area.

9 ☐ The goalkeeper can pick up the ball anywhere on the pitch.

10 ☐ If the referee shows you a yellow card, you have to leave the pitch.

11 ☐ If the referee sees you standing in an offside position, he must blow his whistle.

12 ☐ If you deliberately push an opponent in your own goal area, the other side gets a penalty.

Tennis

13 ☐ When you serve, you have to stand behind the baseline.

14 ☐ If your first serve is out, you can have another try.

15 ☐ You have to let the ball bounce before you hit it.

16 ☐ The ball mustn't bounce more than once on your side of the net before you hit it.

17 ☐ The ball mustn't go higher than five metres.

18 ☐ If you hit your opponent with the ball, you lose the point.

19 ☐ For a ball to be 'in', it must land inside or on the line.

Key...

1 True. 2 True: you must bounce the ball while you run. 3 True: if there's a draw, you have to play extra five-minute periods until someone wins. 4 False: you must do something within five seconds. 5 True. 6 True.
7 True: you *can* touch it accidentally. 8 False: he can go anywhere on the pitch. 9 False: only in his goal area.
10 False: you must go off if he gives you a *red* card. 11 False: only if he thinks you're getting some advantage from it. 12 True (if the referee sees you). 13 True: if your foot touches the line, it's a foot fault. 14 True: you're allowed two serves. 15 False: you can hit it as soon as it's on your side of the net. 16 True. 17 False: there isn't any height limit. 18 False: it's a good way of winning the point. 19 True.

A Types of work

Fill gaps 1–11 in Diagram A and Diagram B. Then read the answers to number 12.

A

B

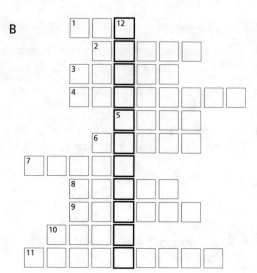

1 ▶ 'I'm a (A) officer. I arrest people who break the (B).'
2 ▶ 'I'm a (A). I type letters and I answer the (B).'
3 ▶ 'I'm an (A). I act in (B) and films.'
4 ▶ 'I'm a (A). I look after (B) in a hospital.'
5 ▶ 'I'm a hotel (A). I (B) with enquiries and reservations.'
6 ▶ 'I'm the accounts (A) for a large company. I look after the company's (B).'
7 ▶ 'I'm a hotel (A). I (B) guests' luggage for them.'
8 ▶ 'I'm a (A). I write children's (B).'
9 ▶ 'I'm a (A). I paint the inside and outside of people's (B).'
10 ▶ 'I'm a (A). I have to (B) a lot of books, and write a lot of essays.'
11 ▶ 'I'm a shop (A). I serve the (B) who come into the shop.'

12 ▼ The speakers all have different (A). They answer the question (B)?'

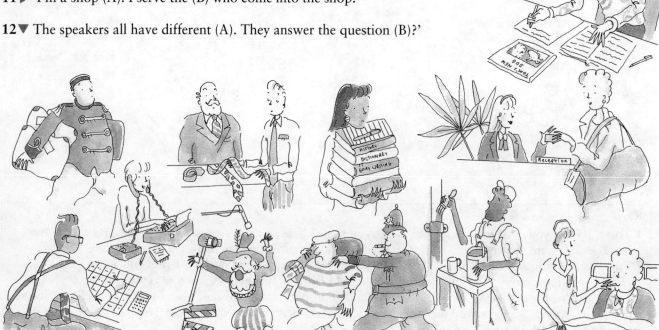

B Careers

Fill the gaps with a verb from the box, in the right form.
Some are used more than once.

apply	look
be	lose
enjoy	retire
get	start
leave	work

1 Last week I .... for a job in a car factory, but I didn't
.... it.

2 – Where do you .... ?

– in a shop. I only .... the job last week.

– Are you .... it?

– No, not much. I'm going to .... at the end of the week.

3 If you're not careful, you'll .... the sack.

4 He .... his job when the factory closed, so he's .... for another one.

5 I'm .... as a taxi driver at the moment.

6 She .... off as a secretary, but she .... soon promoted to sales manager.

And when the director .... in two years' time, she'll probably .... his job.

New words

Use this space to write down new words from the unit, with your own notes and examples.

....
....
....
....
....
....
....
....
....
....
....
....
....

TRANSLATION

Translate into your own language:

1 Have they got any vacancies?
   I'm looking for a job.

   ....
   ....

2 – Does she still work for Shell?
   – No, she retired last year.

   ....
   ....

3 I don't earn very much, but I
   enjoy the work and I get long
   holidays.

   ....
   ....
   ....

4 I'm writing to apply for the job
   you advertised in the *Times*.

   ....
   ....

Now cover up the left-hand side, and translate your sentences back into English.

LISTENING: A security guard

You will hear an interview with a security guard who works
for a company called *Securicor*.

1 Listen to the first part and complete these
   sentences.

   Securicor guards are hired by ....
   ....

   Their job is to guard ....
   ....

   They prevent ....
   ....

2 Before you listen to the second part, try to guess

   how the man would answer these questions.

   Write *Yes* or *No*.

   a Is the work varied?   ....

   b Do you meet people in your job?   ....

   c Is it interesting?   ....

   d Is it well paid?   ....

   e Can you earn overtime pay?   ....

   f Do you have to work at night?   ....

   g Do you get much free time?   ....

3 Listen and check your answers.

SOUND AND SPELLING: Hard and soft *c* and *g*

1 Listen to these words on the tape.
   Hard c: /k/   camera, cost, cut, back, fact
   Soft c: /s/   cent, city, receive, icy, dancing
   Hard g: /g/   garden, gun, pig, foggy, again,
                  ugly
   Soft g: /dʒ/ page, large, judge, changing,
                  pigeon

2 How do you say these words? Mark them
   H (hard) or S (soft). Then listen.

☐	ceiling	☐	figure
☐	orange	☐	secret
☐	copy	☐	agent
☐	capital	☐	piece
☐	fence	☐	apricot
☐	magazine	☐	fridge

3 You will hear four sentences. Cover this
   page, and write them down.

DICTATION

You will hear two of the texts from
Occupations (Classroom Book, page 80).
Listen and write down what you hear.

WRITING SKILLS: Letter writing

1 How we end a letter depends on how we begin it.
Look at the examples in the box.

2 Match the beginnings and endings of
the letters below.
Who's writing to:

a Boyd's? ....

b Susan? ....

c Cosmos? ....

d Tom? ....

Beginning	Ending
Dear Sir Dear Madam Dear Sir/Madam	Yours faithfully
Dear Ms Jones Dear Mr King Dear Mrs Marple	Yours sincerely
Dear Tom Dear Fiona	Best wishes Yours Love

Yours faithfully,
Elizabeth Burke

Yours sincerely,
Douglas Trafford

Yours,
Miranda

The Manager,
Boyd's Bookshop,
15 College Rd.,
Bristol BR4 6LU

Dear Sir/Madam,

   I am writing to complain about
who was extremely rude to me on

Ms P. Williams,
Cosmos Travel,
5 New St.,
Cardiff CF3 2BD

Dear Ms Williams,

   Thank you for
sending

Lots of love,
Don
x x x

Dear Susan,

   I just had to write to
can't stop thinking abo.
such a wonderful time
I want so much to stay

Dear Tom,
   So sorry not to have written for so long,
but I've had rather a hectic few weeks at

3 You have seen this advertisement in the newspaper.
Write a letter asking for more details, and saying
briefly who you are and why you are interested.
Use the letter format given.

WORK ABROAD and learn a
language at the same time. No
experience necessary.
Write for details to:
Interchange, P.O.Box 532,
Amsterdam, The Netherlands.

                              Your address
                                    Date
Address you're
writing to

Dear...

              (Your letter)

Ending

Revision and extension

1 Sentences

Complete the sentences.
Example:
It's getting late. *I must go* home soon.

1 You can stay out late if you like. You
.... come home early.

2 Spanish isn't very difficult – in fact, it's the
.... I've ever learnt.

3 Duck is .... chicken,
but it's cheaper than steak.

4 I'm still looking for my wallet – I
.... yet.

5 – I'm terribly overweight.
– Well, you .... so
much.

6 – Do you like English mustard?
– I don't know. I ....
tried it.

7 You can smoke in the cafeteria, but
.... smoke in the
classrooms.

2 Asking questions

Complete the questions.
Example:
– *Have you finished* your lunch?
– No, I'm still eating it.

1 – .... John or
Richard?
– Richard's taller, I think.

2 – .... wear a suit?
– No you don't. You can wear whatever you like.

3 – .... the way to
the nearest bank?
– Yes. There's one just round the corner.

4 – .... skiing?
– Yes, I love it, but I'm not very good at it.

5 – .... tennis?
– No I haven't, but I've played table-tennis.

6 – .... yet?
– No, they're still asleep.

7 – .... still
.... for *Argos Travel*?
– Yes I am – I'm the assistant manager now.

3 Prepositions

Fill the gaps with prepositions from the box.

1 Have you ever been .... a jazz concert?

2 She resigned .... her old job and now she's
applying .... a new one.

3 I'm looking .... my keys. Have you seen
them anywhere?

4 She studied chemistry .... university.

5 Turn right .... the traffic lights and you'll
see the house .... the end .... the
road.

after	from	out of
at	into	to
for	of	with

6 Please do not throw bottles .... the window.

7 Johnson kicked the ball straight past the goalkeeper
.... the net.

8 I work .... a package tour company. I look
.... the tourists and deal .... any
problems they have.

4 Word order

Put these jumbled sentences in the right order. Remember to begin each
sentence with a capital letter.

Example:
worked hotel ever he a has in ?
Has he ever worked in a hotel?

1 more to they any theatre go don't the .

....

2 you to to time work have what get do ?

....

3 guide working enjoy she as tourist a doesn't .

....

4 and road go right this down turn straight .

....

5 nurses money doctors than more earn .

....

6 think Europe the city in I is beautiful Prague most .

....

5 Writing paragraphs

Write a short paragraph (2 or 3 sentences) on the following:

1 Imagine you've just won some money. Write part of a letter telling a friend the news.

....

....

....

2 What do you do in your free time? Write about one indoor activity and one outdoor activity.

....

....

....

3 Imagine you're a hotel receptionist. Say what you do in your job.

....

....

....

4 What is there to do in your town in the evenings?

....

....

....

19 Narration

A What were they doing?

There was an electricity cut yesterday evening. What do you think these people were doing when it happened? Complete the sentences using the Past continuous.

Spelling of -ing forms
watch (+ ing) → watching
change (¢ + ing) → changing
have (¢ + ing) → having
run (+ n + ing) → running

1 Helen *was writing a letter on her word processor.*

(The screen suddenly went blank.)

2 The Smiths ....

(They missed the end of their programme.)

3 John ....

(He couldn't find his towel in the dark.)

4 Pamela ....

(She finished it by candlelight.)

5 The Browns ....

(Luckily they had a gas cooker.)

6 Lucia ....

(She put on her jumper back to front.)

7 George ....

(He cut himself.)

8 Terry ....

(He had to finish it later.)

9 Karen ....

(What a pity! She was winning, too!)

B Short stories

Tell stories based on the information in the table. For each story, choose one item from A and one item from B. Say when it happened, and what happened next.

Example:

I was driving to work yesterday morning when I felt a sudden pain in my leg. I stopped the car quickly and got out, and saw a bee on the driver's seat.

A	B
wait for a train	smell smoke
get into the bath	hear someone say 'Hello!'
cook breakfast	hear a shot
walk in a forest	lose [my/her/his ...] balance
drive to work	see the headline in the paper
practise the piano	look at [my/her/his ...] watch
paint the ceiling	feel a sudden pain

1 ....

....

....

....

2 ....

....

....

....

3 ....

....

....

....

C ...-ing ...-ing ...

What do you remember about the street scene in Unit 18 of the Classroom Book? Use *two* expressions from the box (changing them to *-ing* forms) to complete each sentence.

carry two suitcases	sing
carry some bricks	sit by the road
come out of a hotel	sit in a café
dig a hole in the road	stand by a piano
drink coffee	stand by a car
look at the engine	stand on the pavement
play a saxophone	wear a helmet

1 There was a workman   *standing on the pavement, carrying some bricks.* ....

2 There was a porter ....

3 A young woman was ....

4 In the street there was a man ....

5 Upstairs there was a woman ....

6 A mechanic was ....

7 Two men were ....

TRANSLATION

Translate into your own language:

1 – How did you break your leg?
  – I fell off a ladder.

....

....

2 We first met in Paris. I was
  visiting my uncle at the time.

....

....

3 I was sitting at a table having a cup of
  coffee when someone shouted 'Fire!'

....

....

4 He wasn't feeling well, so he left.

....

Now cover up the left-hand side, and translate your sentences back into English.

LISTENING: Two stories

You will hear two stories. Story A is about a wedding.
Story B is about football hooligans.

1 Before you listen, guess which words you think
appear in each story. Mark them A or B.

	carriage		reception
	embarrassing		supporters
	frightened		terrifying
	groom		underground
	noise		video
	platform		wallet

Now listen to the tape, and check your answers.

2 Listen again and complete the stories.

Story A: The speaker went to a friend's ....
They made a .... of their ....,
and later they .... him round to watch it.
While watching it, he noticed the .... of the
.... stealing someone's .... It
was very ....

Story B: The speaker was sitting in .... when
a crowd of .... got in. First they made a lot of
.... Then they started rocking the
.... She felt very ...., and got
out as soon as the .... opened. Then she burst
into ....

PRONUNCIATION: Intonation: questions

1 We usually use *rising intonation*:
  – in Yes/No questions
  – if we want something repeated
  We usually use *falling intonation*:
  – in Wh- questions
  Listen to the examples.

1 Is Mary at home? ⤴
Yes, she is. ⤵
2 What's the time? ⤵
About six o'clock. ⤵
3 I come from Portsmouth. ⤵
Where? ⤴

2 Mark these sentences with ⤵ or ⤴.

  a – Can you ski?
    – Yes, I can.
  b – My car's broken down.
    – Oh, has it really?
  c – My name's Mifanwy.
    – Pardon?
  d – Did you see the film last night?
    – Yes, I did.
    – What did you think of it?

Now listen to the tape. Then practise saying
the sentences.

DICTATION

You will hear part of the text from *Setting a
scene* (Classroom Book, page 88).
Listen and write down what you hear.

READING: Bad luck

Here are two stories about bad luck. Put the sentences in the right order.

Superstition

1 ..*H*..　2 ....　3 ....　4 ....　5 ....

6 ....　7 ....　8 ....　9 ....

A　'I'll never be superstitious again,' she said.

B　Then she stepped off the pavement to avoid walking under a ladder and a bicycle knocked her over.

C　She believed that Friday was an unlucky day, and that thirteen was an unlucky number.

D　It was Friday the thirteenth.

E　One day she stopped to stroke a black cat on a wall and it scratched her face.

F　Then she looked at the calendar.

G　She arrived home with her face bleeding and her leg bruised.

H　Sue was very superstitious.

I　She thought that black cats brought good luck, and never walked under a ladder if she could help it.

The Thief

1 ..*C*..　2 ....　3 ....　4 ....

5 ....　6 ....　7 ....　8 ....

A　Now they could do whatever they liked: no one could prove anything.

B　They knew!

C　The train came in, and Jake followed two elderly women into the nearest compartment.

D　Jake quietly took the bag out of his pocket and dropped it out of the window.

E　It was then that he saw the *No Smoking* sign in the window.

F　As they left the station, he noticed one of the women staring at him over her newspaper.

G　He had a bag of stolen jewels in his pocket, and he lit up a cigarette to steady his nerves.

H　Then, to his horror, he heard them whispering something about calling the guard.

*Adapted from **Micro Stories** by Josephine Jones (Wida Software)*

20 People

A Physical appearance

Use the words in the boxes to describe the people in the story.

I got on the train, and found my seat. There was only one other person in the compartment. He *was a short man in his 30s with curly black hair and a moustache. He was wearing a brown raincoat.* Just before the train left the station, a woman came into our compartment and sat down opposite me. She ....
....
....

At the next station, an elderly man got in and sat in the corner. He
....
....
....
....

The next station was mine. I got off the train and telephoned Mrs Chadwick. 'I'll come and meet you in five minutes,' she said. 'How will I recognise you?' 'Well,' I said, 'I'm ....
....
....
....
....,

black	moustache
short	30s
curly hair	brown
raincoat	

green	tall	short
fair	sunglasses	
hair	dress	20s

beard	blue	grey
walking stick	70s	
short	bald	eyes

Describe yourself.

B Character adjectives

Match the sentences with the words in the box.

☐	shy	☐	generous
☐	selfish	1	friendly
☐	modest	☐	self-confident
☐	mean	☐	bad-tempered
☐	honest	☐	easy-going
☐	lazy	☐	hard-working

1 ... always smiles and says hello when we meet.
2 ... doesn't like giving away money.
3 ... gets angry quite a lot.
4 ... is afraid to speak to strangers.
5 ... isn't afraid to speak to strangers.
6 ... usually stays late at the office.
7 ... always tells the truth.
8 ... doesn't get upset if things go wrong.
9 ... doesn't work very hard.
10 ... always brings you a little present.
11 ... doesn't boast.
12 ... is only interested in himself/herself.

New words

Use this space to write down new words from the unit, with your own notes and examples.

....
....
....
....
....
....
....
....
....
....
....
....
....
....

TRANSLATION

Translate into your own language:

1 – She's still in her 20s.
– Is she? She looks older than that.

....

....

2 He was a tall, thin man with long,
fair hair and a moustache, and he
always wore a leather jacket.

....

....

....

3 – Do you always wear glasses?
– No, only for driving.

....

....

4 He's one of the most generous
people I've ever met.

....

....

Now cover up the left-hand side, and translate your sentences back into English.

LISTENING: Famous people

You will hear three people describing (1) Queen Victoria,
(2) Napoleon and (3) Indira Gandhi.

1 Here are some of the things they say.
Before you listen: Which phrases do you think go with
each person? Write V, N or G.

a ☐ very impressive looking

b ☐ always wore black

c ☐ always wore a uniform

d ☐ didn't often laugh

e ☐ wore a three-pointed hat

f ☐ lived to a very old age

g ☐ had a very striking face

h ☐ a very peaceful looking person

i ☐ hair tied in a tight bun

j ☐ was dark-skinned and had greying hair

k ☐ had dark hair and dark eyes

l ☐ had a small mouth and quite a pointed chin

2 Listen to the tape and check your answers.

SOUND AND SPELLING:
Long and short vowels

1 Listen to these words on the tape.

Words with short vowels

bad	get	sit	stop	fun
rabbit	getting	dinner	stopped	sunny

Words with long vowels

late	hide	hope	amuse
latest	hiding	hotel	used

2 Here are some words that you probably
don't know. How do you think they are
said? Mark them S (short) or L (long).
Then listen to the tape.

☐	mute	☐	glutton
☐	coping	☐	scraper
☐	scram	☐	flitted
☐	pane	☐	inducing
☐	strive	☐	spottiest
☐	petty	☐	refinery

3 You will hear four sentences. Write them
down.

DICTATION

You will hear three parts of the reading text
from *The Dream Game* (Classroom Book,
page 93).

Listen and write down what you hear.

WRITING SKILLS: Relative clauses (1)

1 Here are two parts of a letter written by a foreign student in Paris.

| I'm staying with my uncle. He lives just outside Paris. He's got a large house, with a beautiful garden. | My uncle is quite rich. He works for Inter Export. It's a large company based in Paris. |

We can join the sentences in each paragraph like this:

| I'm staying with my uncle, **who** lives just outside Paris. He's got a large house, with a beautiful garden. | My uncle is quite rich. He works for Inter Export, **which** is a large company based in Paris. |

We use *who* to talk about people.
We use *which* to talk about things.
Before *who* or *which* we write a comma (,).

2 These sentences all have mistakes. Rewrite them correctly.

a I live in Stenton, it's a small village near Cambridge.

....

....

b I've got three sisters, which are all older than me.

....

....

c I've got a younger brother. Who's in the army.

....

....

d Pandas, which they only eat bamboo, are becoming very rare.

....

....

| She's studying art here. |
| It's a kind of sausage. |
| It still isn't very good. |
| They're also staying in Paris. |
| It was built in the 70s. |
| It's about 200 km south of here. |

3 Here are some more sentences from the student's letter. Fill the gaps with information from the box. Use *who* or *which*.

a I'm sending you a picture of the Pompidou Centre, ...

What do you think of it?

b Last night I met some old schoolfriends, ... We went out

for a meal together.

c I had a very interesting dish called *andouillette*, ...

d George sends you his best wishes. He's staying in Lyon, ...

e I'm spending a lot of time with a girl called Mona, ...

I met her at a party last weekend.

f I'm doing everything I can to improve my French, ...

21 Prediction

A Will, might & won't

Choose topics from the box, and make three predictions for the next ten years:
one with *will (probably)*, one with *might* and one with *(probably) won't*.

Example: *my life*

*I'll probably get married. I might go and live abroad. I probably
won't have any children.*

my life
politics
sport
my family
television
science

1 Topic: ....

....

....

2 Topic: ....

....

....

3 Topic: ....

....

....

B Questions with 'will'

Ask questions with *will*. Some are Yes/No questions, and some are Wh- questions.

Examples:

Mexico City might win tonight, or they might not. → *Will Mexico City win tonight?*

There might be 20 people at the party. Or 30. Or ... → *How many people will there be at the party?*

1 The train might arrive at 2.00, or at 2.30, or ...

....

2 It might be windy tomorrow, or it might not.

....

3 There might be a general election this year, or there might not.

....

4 You might be at home, or at work, or ...

....

5 I might see you again tomorrow, or next week, or ...

....

6 They might lend us the money, or they might not.

....

7 The ticket might cost me £10, or £20, or ...

....

C If & unless

Write sentences with *if* or *unless* based on these pieces of advice.

unless = if ... not ...
If you post it now, it'll probably get there on time.
If you *don't* post it now, it won't get there on time.
Unless you post it now, it won't get there on time.

Examples:

You ought to complain about it.   → *If you complain, they'll give you a new one.*
You should book a seat for the concert. → *You won't get in unless you book a seat.*

1 You should wear a raincoat when you go out.

....

2 You ought to leave before dark.

....

3 You ought to apologise.

....

4 You should phone your parents.

....

5 You should go to bed early tonight.

....

6 Don't forget his birthday.

....

7 You ought to have a holiday.

....

D Predictions with 'going to'

Complete each item with a prediction with *going to*.

Example: There isn't a cloud in the sky. ...

It's going to be a beautiful day.
It's not going to rain.
It's going to be a cold night.
There are going to be lots of stars tonight.

1 Look at all those dark clouds in the sky. ...

....

2 She's pregnant. She's ...

....

3 Oh dear. Have you got a tissue? I think ...

....

4 I've eaten too many chocolates. I think ...

....

5 That plane's flying much too low. ...

....

6 You haven't done enough work for your exam. ...

....

7 And he's a long way in front of the others now! ...

....

8 He's had a car accident. But don't worry – ...

....

TRANSLATION

Translate into your own language:

1 They'll probably just ask you a few
  questions. And they might take
  your photograph.

....

....

....

2 – How long will it take to get there?
  – About a quarter of an hour if we
    walk quickly.

....

....

....

3 I haven't got any money on me –
  I'll have to write you a cheque.

....

....

Now cover up the left-hand side, and translate your sentences back into English.

LISTENING: Driving test

You will hear a woman explaining what to
expect when taking a driving test in Britain.

1 Here are some things the instructor will say
  during the test. In what order does the
  woman mention them? Listen and number
  the remarks from 1 to 7.

2 Listen again and answer these questions.
  a Where do you take the driving test?
  b What is the first thing you do when you
    get in the car?
  c What does the instructor have with him?
  d What does the pink paper mean?

PRONUNCIATION: Contrastive stress

1 We can change the meaning of a sentence by changing the
  stress. Listen to the examples.

> I like playing <u>football</u>.
> I like playing **foot**ball.
> *(but not tennis)*
> I like **play**ing football.
> *(but not watching it)*
> <u>I</u> like playing football.
> *(but my brother doesn't)*

2 How do you say these sentences? Underline the main
  stress

  a She was a maths teacher.
    (not a history teacher)

  b She was a maths teacher.
    (she works in a library now)

  c My mother usually gets up early.
    (but the rest of us stay in bed)

  d My mother usually gets up early.
    (but not always)

  e I didn't see him yesterday.
    (it was three days ago)

  f I didn't see him yesterday.
    (I spoke to him on the phone)

  Now listen to the tape.

DICTATION

You will hear two parts of the text from *What will it be
like?* (Classroom Book, page 94).

Listen and write down what you hear.

READING: Star gazing

1 What can people born under these four star signs expect this week?
Write the first letter of each star sign L (= Libra), S, P and/or T.

Who might expect ...

a a romantic evening? ....

b to hear about other
people's problems? ....

c to hear from a long
lost friend? ....

d an interesting week
at work ....

e to win an argument? ....

f money troubles? ....

g to get some money? ....

h a plan to go wrong? ....

i something nice to
happen on Tuesday? ....

j a problem with
someone in the
family? ....

2 Which horoscope would you

a most like to be yours? ....

b least like to be yours? ....

YOUR FUTURE IN THE STARS

Paul Zak reveals what the week has in store

LIBRA

23 September-21 October

If you've been on holiday this week, you might find that you don't want to go back to work – who does? But an unexpected visit will cheer you up, and there may be a letter or a long-distance phone call from a relative or friend. Someone close to you suddenly changes their mind, and you find you've won a long-standing argument without saying a word. At home, something you've planned doesn't work out, but don't worry – everything will turn out all right in the end.

☆ Be careful what you say on Friday.

PISCES

20 February-20 March

You'll be occupied with worries about your home and family this week. You may be having problems paying the bills, or perhaps someone isn't doing all they can to help around the house. It's a problem that can be solved – but it's up to you to do it. This would also be a good time to sit down and write all those letters you've been putting off. Friends might bring their problems to you too: you can help, but you should sort out your own problems first.

☆ A lucky break on Tuesday.

SAGITTARIUS

23 November-21 December

Lots of things go right this week. A friend you haven't seen for years turns up out of the blue, and you sort out an old family quarrel. Your love-life goes well too – you can look forward to a great night out, and something you've been dreaming of for years actually comes true. At work, someone tries to make things difficult for you, but who cares? There are good times ahead, so forget about work and enjoy yourself.

☆ Don't make any big decisions on Monday.

TAURUS

21 April-21 May

If you're planning to spend your money having fun this week, better forget it – you've got some big bills coming. But there's no need to worry: if you're careful, you should be able to sort things out fairly quickly – and you might even end up richer than when you started. At work, you have an opportunity to show what you can do: make the most of it.

☆ An enjoyable meeting on Tuesday.

22 Around the world

A On the map

Write the missing words in the diagram. Then complete sentence number 12.

1 .... Victoria is in East Africa; .... Superior is in Canada. (4)
2 Asia is one; Europe is another; Africa is another. (9)
3 Vesuvius is a ....; so is Etna; and Popocatepetl; and Krakatoa. (7)
4 The Danube is a ....; so is the Thames; and the Amazon. (5)
5 The Niagara falls are on the U.S.–Canada ....(6)
6 An area full of trees, such as the Black .... in Germany. (6)
7 The Atlantic, for example; or the Pacific; or the Indian. (5)
8 Fuji, for example; or the Matterhorn; or Kilimanjaro. (8)
9 A dry region, such as the Sahara, the Gobi, and the Kalahari. (6)
10 Sri Lanka is an ....; so is Cyprus; and Tahiti. (6)
11 San Francisco is on the West .... of the U.S.A. (5)

12▼ Answers 1–11 are all part of the ....

B A good place to visit

A friend has asked you to recommend a good place to go for a holiday in your country. Write part of a letter, in which you answer these questions:

What's the place called? Where is it?

What's the surrounding area like?

What can you do there?

What's the weather like?

What's the best time of year to go there?

....
....
....
....
....
....
....
....

C International quiz

The answers to all the questions are countries, nationalities or languages.

1 Which countries are these the capital cities of?

   a Edinburgh ....

   b Bangkok ....

   c Ankara ....

   d Budapest ....

   e Dublin ....

   f Vienna ....

2 What nationality are the speakers?

   a 'I'm from Rio de Janiero.' ....

   b 'I'm from Lisbon.' ....

   c 'I'm from Toronto.' ....

   d 'I'm from Johannesburg.' ....

   e 'I'm from Warsaw.' ....

   f 'I'm from Copenhagen.' ....

3 What languages do these words come from?

   a karate ....

   b pizza ....

   c champagne ....

   d sauna ....

   e perestroika ....

4 Here is *Do you speak ...?* in six different languages. What languages are they?

   a ¿Hablas español? ....

   b Spreek jij Nederlands? ....

   c Sprechen Sie deutsch? ....

   d هل تتكلم العربية ؟ ....

   e Μιλάτε ελληνικά; ....

   f 你会说中文吗？ ....

New words

Use this space to write down new words from the unit, with your own notes and examples.

....

....

....

....

....

....

....

....

....

....

....

....

TRANSLATION

Translate into your own language:

1 Her first language is Turkish, but she also speaks Arabic and Chinese.

....

....

2 No wonder I feel hot. The temperature's nearly 40° in here.

....

....

3 It's a large industrial town not far from the coast.

....

....

4 It's often quite windy here in the winter, but it hardly ever rains.

....

....

Now cover up the left-hand side, and translate your sentences back into English.

LISTENING: Living in a hot climate

You will hear a woman talking about the climate in the Arabian Gulf. Look at these questions. Then listen and note down the woman's answers. Are there any questions she *doesn't* answer?

1 Is it always hot in the Arabian Gulf?

....

2 Which are the hottest months?

....

3 When is the coolest time of year?

....

4 Is it humid?

....

5 Does it ever rain?

....

6 Are most buildings air-conditioned?

....

7 Is it too hot to drive a car?

....

8 Do you ever need warm clothes?

....

9 Is the sea pleasant to swim in?

....

SOUND AND SPELLING: Words with *s*

1 Listen to these words on the tape.
   /s/: sit, smoke, science, square
   /s/: lesson, passing, possible, escape, disturb, whisper
   /s/: class, less, makes, lights, maps, laughs
   /z/: easy, losing, wiser, thousand
   /z/: apples, goes, mends, legs, matches

2 How do you say these words? Mark them s or z. Then listen to the tape.

☐	press	☐	buys
☐	busy	☐	scream
☐	coughs	☐	climbs
☐	messy	☐	listen
☐	princes	☐	please
☐	princess	☐	trousers

3 You will hear eight words. How do you spell them? Write them down.

DICTATION

You will hear part of the text from *Visiting time* (Classroom Book, page 99).

Listen and write down what you hear.

WRITING SKILLS: Relative clauses (2)

1 Look at this information about India.

Bombay is one of India's main sea ports. (**It**'s on the west coast.)

Jawaharlal Nehru died in 1964. (**He** was the first prime minister of India.)

200 kilometres from the capital Delhi is the town of Agra. (The Taj Mahal was built **there** in 1653.)

The best time to visit Agra is November-February. (The weather's not too hot **then**.)

We can join these ideas together using relative clauses:

Bombay, **which** is on the west coast, is one of India's main sea ports.	Jawaharlal Nehru, **who** was the first prime minister of India, died in 1964.	200 kilometres from the capital Delhi is the town of Agra, **where** the Taj Mahal was built in 1653.	The best time to visit Agra is November-February, **when** the weather's not too hot.

2 Join the ideas in brackets ( ) to the main sentence using a relative clause.

a Jakarta has a population of about seven million. (It's the capital of Indonesia.)

....
....
....

b The Cape Verde Islands have been independent since 1975. (They used to be a Portuguese colony.)

....
....
....

c In the Square there is a statue of Charles I. (He was King of England from 1625 to 1649.)

....
....
....

d In Alaska it can be dangerous to go out in winter. (The temperature often falls below −30°.)

....
....
....

3 Join these ideas together so that they make a paragraph of four or five sentences. Use *who*, *which*, *where* and *and*.

If you have time, you should visit the Parrot Café. It's in a small side street behind the harbour. It's the oldest café in the town. It's very popular with fishermen. They sit there all day playing cards. The owner is in his 80s. He's a retired sea captain. Next to the Parrot Café there's a small museum. You can see treasure from an old sailing ship there. It sank near the town in the 17th century.

....
....
....
....
....
....
....
....
....
....
....
....

23 Duration

A For or since?

Fill the gaps with *for* or *since*.

1 I stayed there .... two weeks when I was a student. And .... then we've gone there for our summer holiday every year.

2 We've known each other .... most of our lives, but we've only been married .... a few months.

3 Nigeria was a British colony .... more than 50 years. It has been independent .... 1960.

4 I only slept .... four hours last night – I've been up .... five o'clock this morning. I'm so tired, I think I could sleep .... a week.

5 She's been driving .... her 17th birthday, and she's now 31, so she's been driving .... 14 years.

6 He hasn't changed much. He's been living in the same house .... the 50s; he's been doing the same job .... nearly 40 years; and he's been driving the same car .... I was a boy. And he's had that moustache .... his early 20s.

B Talking about duration

I've	had that dog	for	six months.
He's	lived here		five years.
			a long time.
We've	been living here	since	January.
They've	been learning French		1965.
			last summer.

Rewrite these sentences using *for* or *since*.
Examples:

He turned on the TV half an hour ago. → *He's been watching the TV for half an hour.*
I got this cold on Friday. → *I've had this cold since Friday.*

1 I met him at my birthday party.

....

2 She went to sleep a long time ago.

....

3 They started learning Arabic last autumn.

....

4 We got divorced six months ago.

....

5 I started reading this book yesterday lunchtime.

....

6 She got her guitar for Christmas.

....

7 He started wearing glasses five years ago.

....

C How long...?

Continue these remarks with questions with *How long ...?*

Examples:

I see you've got a dog now.	→	*How long have you had it?*
Oh, so they've moved to London, have they?	→	*How long have they been living there?*

1 Oh, so you know Kate, do you?

....

2 I see he's got a cold.

....

3 I didn't know they were staying in this hotel.

....

4 Oh, so he plays the piano, does he?

....

5 Her Spanish is very good.

....

6 That's a lovely coat you're wearing.

....

7 I didn't know she was in Italy.

....

D Autobiography

Write a few sentences about your past life. Say what you did, and say when and for how long.

Example:

I was born in 1965. I spent the first five years of my life in Oxford. Then we lived in London for 12 years. I went to secondary school from 1976 till 1982. Then I studied law at college for five years. I left college in 1987, and spent a year travelling. Since then, I've been working as a solicitor.

> **I spent** three years (**working**) in a bank.
> I worked in a bank **for** three years.
> I worked in a bank **from** 1986 **to/till** 1989.

....

....

....

....

....

....

....

....

....

....

TRANSLATION

Translate into your own language:

1 – You look exhausted.
– Yes, I've been up since 6 o'clock.

....

....

2 – How long have you known each other?
– Ages. We were at school together.

....

....

3 She's very fit. She spends at least
two hours a day doing exercises.

....

....

4 I was there from 9 o'clock till
lunchtime.

....

....

Now cover up the left hand side, and translate your sentences back into English.

LISTENING: 24 hours

You will hear someone saying how she spent a typical day.

1 Listen and complete the table.

Activity	How long?
a work	
b travel	
c meals	
d talking	
e reading	
f TV	
g sleep	

2 Now listen again and answer these questions.

a What is Mary's occupation?

....

b How many children has she got?

....

c Does she live a long way from the shops?

....

d What is the main meal of her day?

....

e What kind of books does she read most?

....

f How does she feel at the end of the day?

....

PRONUNCIATION: Dialogues

Look at these dialogues.

1 Underline the main stress in each sentence.

2 Mark each sentence with an arrow to show rising ⤴ or falling ⤵ intonation.

3 Which sounds are reduced to /ə/ ?

Dialogue A

– I'm going to Spain next week.
– Are you? Who are you going with?
– Mary.
– Who?

Dialogue B

– Would you like to come to the cinema tonight?
– No, I'm afraid I can't. I'm busy tonight.
– Are you free tomorrow, then?
– No, I'm busy tomorrow, too.

Dialogue C

– Have you ever been to Malaysia?
– No I haven't, but I've been to Thailand.
– Oh. Were you there on holiday?
– No, not on holiday. It was a business trip.

Now listen and check your answers.

DICTATION

You will hear three parts of the text from *A Slice of life* (Classroom Book, page 103).
Listen and write down what you hear.

READING: General knowledge quiz

How good is your general knowledge? Try these questions (choose a, b, c or d).
Then check your answers in the key.

1 In 1927, Charles Lindbergh completed the first solo flight across the Atlantic. He was in the air for about
   a 9 hours   b 17 hours
   c 25 hours   d 33 hours

2 Tokyo has been the capital city of Japan since
   a 1718   b 1768   c 1868   d 1918

3 Horses usually live for between 20 and 35 years, but they can live for as long as
   a 40–45 years   b 50–55 years
   c 60–65 years   d 70–75 years

4 The wheel is one of civilisation's oldest and most useful inventions. But how long have people been using wheeled vehicles?
   a less than 3000 years   b 3,000–4,000 years
   c 4,000–5,000 years   d more than 5000 years

5 In 1961, the Soviet astronaut Yuri Gagarin became the first man in Space. His flight lasted for
   a less than 2 hours   b 12 hours
   c 3 days   d more than 5 days

6 In Switzerland, women have had the vote since
   a 1881   b 1911   c 1941   d 1971

7 When the Sun's light reaches the Earth, it has been travelling for
   a 8½ seconds   b 85 seconds
   c 8½ minutes   d 85 minutes

8 Singapore is one of the world's smallest countries (620 square km). It's been an independent state since
   a 1945   b 1955   c 1965   d 1975

9 Agatha Christie's play *The Mousetrap* is London's longest running play. It's been running continuously since
   a 1952   b 1962   c 1972   d 1982

10 At the North Pole, it's daylight for six months of the year. But which six months?
   a   from mid-December to mid-June
   b   from mid-March to mid-September
   c   from mid-June to mid-December
   d   from mid-September to mid-March

Key

1 d The flight, from Long Island, New York, to Paris, France, was 5810 km long. Lindbergh won a $25,000 prize.

2 c Before that Kyoto was the capital.

3 c The record is held by 'Old Billy', a working horse from Lancashire, England, who lived for 62 years (1760-1822).

4 d The wheel was invented by the Sumerians in about 3300 BC. These were solid wheels: wheels with spokes appeared 1,400 years later.

5 a Gagarin's rocket left the Soviet Union on 12 April 1961, went once round the Earth , and landed again 108 minutes later. It travelled at a height of 320 km and a speed of 28,000 kph.

6 d Male voters decided to allow women to vote in a referendum held in February 1971.

7 c Light travels at 18 million km per minute, and the Sun is 150 million km from the Earth.

8 c Formerly a British Colony, Singapore was part of Malaysia from 1963 until 1965.

9 a It's a major tourist attraction. The identity of the murderer is a well kept secret.

10 b And then it's dark from mid-September to mid-March.

24 But is it art?

A People and places

Which people and places do you associate with the
following? Fill the spaces with words from the box.
You'll need to use some words more than once.

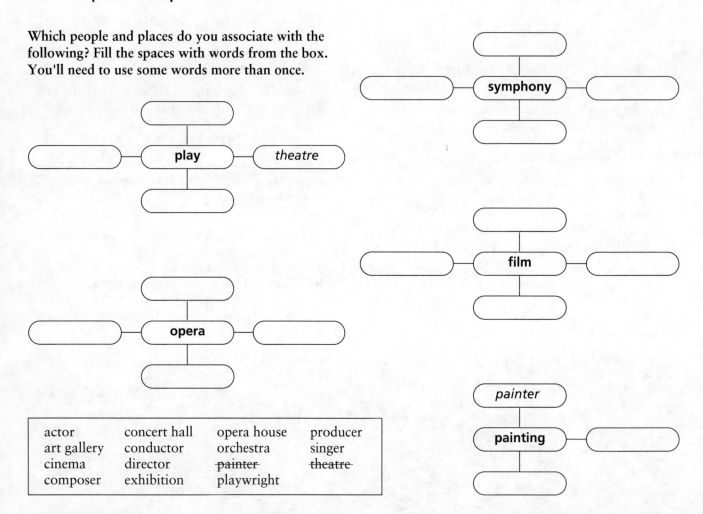

actor	concert hall	opera house	producer
art gallery	conductor	orchestra	singer
cinema	director	~~painter~~	~~theatre~~
composer	exhibition	playwright	

B Personally speaking

Have you seen any good films recently? What's your taste in paintings? Are you reading anything at the moment? Who's your favourite singer? Write about yourself.

At the moment I'm reading 'The Grapes of Wrath', by John Steinbeck. It's about an American family who have to leave their farm and go to California looking for work.	*Last week I went to see 'Metropolis', which is an old science fiction film about a city in the future. It was very good.*	*Hank Wangford is a country and western singer. I like his music very much and I've got three of his records.*

....
....
....
....
....
....
....
....
....
....

New words

Use this space to write down new words from the unit, with your own notes and examples.

TRANSLATION

Translate into your own language:

1 Picasso was born in Spain, but he painted most of his best-known pictures in France.

....
....
....

2 What's this poem about? I don't understand it.

....
....

3 Jaws III is on at the cinema tonight. Shall we go and see it together?

....
....

4 I like this music. I find it very relaxing.

....
....

Now cover up the left-hand side, and translate your sentences back into English.

LISTENING: Choosing a painting

You will hear someone talking about the pictures in Classroom Book, page 108–9:

A *Street Scene*
B *Woman's Head with Sombrero*
C *Painting 1937*
D *Landschaft am Meer*
E *Circus Girl*
F *Icarus*

1 Here are some of the comments he makes:

   – I'd find it rather disturbing
   – It's a very warm painting
   – Suitable for a hall
   – Interesting for a few moments
   – I'd grow bored with it rather quickly
   – A very peaceful painting

   Which pictures do you think each comment is about?

2 Listen and decide which pictures he would put on a wall in his home. (Write ✔, ✗ or ? in the table.)
   Add the comments above in their correct places.

	✔, ✗ or ?	Comment
A		
B		
C		
D		
E		
F		

3 Which painting is the man's favourite? ....

SOUND AND SPELLING: Words with *th*

1 Listen to these words on the tape.
   /θ/: thick, thought, three, thing
   /θ/: author, athletics, death, path, fifth, south, bath
   /ð/: this, them, then, therefore
   /ð/: other, father, southern, either, bathe

2 How do you say these words? Mark them /θ/ or /ð/. Then listen to the tape.

☐	earth	☐	thumb
☐	theirs	☐	mouth
☐	brother	☐	these
☐	months	☐	neither
☐	northern	☐	breathe
☐	leather	☐	cloth
☐	both	☐	clothes

3 You will hear six sentences. Write down any words you hear with *th* in them.

DICTATION

You will hear part of the story *The Night in the Hotel* (Classroom Book, page 110, line 30 to line 35).

Listen and write down what you hear.

WRITING SKILLS: Sequence (3)

left school			went abroad	caught malaria	came home
... at school	worked in a factory		lived abroad		
	← a few months →		← a year →		

1 The sentences below show different ways of organising information from the table above:

A He left school, **and then** got a job in a factory.
 After leaving
 After he left | school, he worked in a factory for a few months.

B He went abroad for a year. But **before that** he worked in a factory to earn some money.
 Before | he went
 | going | abroad, he worked in a factory to earn some money.

C He left school, and a few months **later** he went abroad.
 A few months **after** leaving school, he went abroad.

D **While** | he was living
 | living | abroad, he caught malaria and nearly died.

2 Correct the mistakes in these sentences:

a A few weeks after that he bought a new motorbike, he was injured in a road accident.
b She moved to Buenos Aires to work as a sculptor. Two years after, she had her first exhibition.
c Before to leave the house, I checked that all the lights were switched off.
d Two years after he joining the firm, he was promoted to manager.
e While staying in India. She visited the Taj Mahal several times.

3 Join these sentences to make a coherent story. Make any changes you think are necessary.

She said goodbye to her friends.	....
She went back to the hotel.	....
Fortunately there was no-one at the desk.	....
She quickly took the key for Room 24.	....
She took the lift to the second floor.	....
She put her ear to the keyhole and listened carefully.	....
She opened the door.	....
She slipped quietly into the room.	....
She switched the light on.	....
She found what she was looking for.	....
The book was in the wardrobe, under some shirts.	....
She looked quickly through it.	....
She put the book back in the wardrobe.	....
She left the room.	....

Revision and extension

1 Verb forms

Write the correct form of the verbs.
Example:
They **'ve been** (be) married for 10 years.

1 We .... (spend) most of yesterday
  evening .... (play) cards.
2 He .... (stand) by the swimming
  pool when someone .... (come) up
  behind him and .... (push) him
  into the water.
3 She .... (play) for years, so I
  expect she .... (win) the match
  tomorrow.
4 Unless you .... (leave) me alone, I
  .... (call) the police.
5 I saw a little girl .... (sit) on the
  floor .... (play) with some
  wooden bricks. She .... (sing) to
  herself.
6 Oh dear! I think I .... (be) sick.

2 Asking questions

Complete the questions.
Example:
– How long *has he been* here?
– Not long. He arrived a few minutes ago.

1 – How much ....?
  – They'll pay you $20 an hour.
2 – How much .... that jacket?
  – Since Christmas. My sister gave it to me.
3 – What ....?
  – He's quite short and he wears glasses.
4 – I was talking to Ali just now.
  – Oh yes? What ....
  about?
5 – What .... in
  Malaysia?
  – It's hot and humid, and it rains quite a lot.
6 – How long ....
  private lessons?
  – Oh, for about a year now.
7 – What .... that
  picture?
  – I like it. The colours are beautiful.

3 Prepositions

Fill the gaps with prepositions from the box.

1 I was driving .... the road when I saw an
  old friend standing .... the bus stop.
2 She isn't very old – I think she's still ....
  her fifties.
3 When you arrive .... the airport you'll
  have to go .... customs.
4 It usually rains .... the coast, but it stays
  dry .... the mountains.

along	from	since	for
at	in	to	on
by	of	through	until

5 – I've been waiting .... nearly an hour.
  – That's nothing. I've been here 9
  o'clock this morning.
6 He works .... 8 in the morning
  .... 6 in the evening, and then he goes
  .... an evening class.
7 The picture .... the woman's face is
  .... Picasso.

4 Word order

Put these jumbled sentences in the right order. Remember to begin each sentence with a capital letter.

Example:

time of television a they watching lot spend .
They spend a lot of time watching television.

1 lunch they arrived telegram having the were while .

....

2 hair a dark with woman long tall she's .

....

3 home it to long take will how get ?

....

4 old 25 about is her years brother .

....

5 early is visit time the the Scotland to best summer .

....

6 hurry you ticket don't get if a might you not .

....

5 Writing paragraphs

Write a short paragraph (2 or 3 sentences) on the following:

1 Describe a past or present leader of your country.

....

....

....

2 Write about a favourite picture or book. Say why you like it.

....

....

....

3 How much time do you spend watching TV? What kind of programmes do you watch?

....

....

....

4 What do you think will happen in the world next week? Make three predictions.

....

....

....

Tapescripts

Unit 13 The most and the least

1 A Well, I don't think I'm all that musical, um but I play cello, saxophone, banjo, recorder and flute, um as well as a little guitar, so I enjoy playing a lot and love singing as well.

B When I was a young boy I played the piano for a few years, but I gave it up when I was about eleven and – Well, I've not played a musical instrument since.

C I learnt to play the piano when I was at school, and also the recorder. I carried on playing the piano for quite a while, but then stopped, sadly, but I have always sung in, in – I've always enjoyed singing.

2 A I'm afraid I only speak English, and a little school French, 'O' level French – um I only really speak, speak English.

B I've got a Spanish father and as a boy I learnt both Spanish and English. I also can speak French quite well and Italian, and I'm not bad at German either.

C I learnt French and German at school, but wasn't very good, but good enough to be able to go to France or Germany and get by and be able to have a conversation.

3 A Oh, I've travelled a lot – um I've been to most of the countries in Europe, um I've also been to Canada and at the same time went to the United States of America, and also down to Mexico, which was lovely.

B I'm sorry to say I've never ever been outside Britain. I must do it sometime.

C I've been very lucky, because my parents worked for one of the airlines, and I've been able to travel. I've travelled to Australia and to Japan, and last year we went to China.

Unit 14 Living in London

1 Well, I like living in London, mainly because I live right in the centre. If I want to go to a theatre, I can leave my house about 15 minutes before the show starts, and walk to the theatre. I can do the same with a cinema. In the morning, I can get up, I can go into Soho and buy fresh croissants and coffee – and generally there is a wonderful cosmopolitan air about the whole place.

2 I don't like living in London at all. We've got a very small garden with a railway at the bottom, so it's noisy. Aeroplanes go over every two minutes, so you can't sit outside because there are trains and planes, and it's very dirty as well. My journey to work is horrendous, because I get into a packed tube, it's packed with people. We never get a seat, people are extremely rude and push in front of you to get a seat, and the same returning home in the evenings. I think living out in the country must be much nicer.

Unit 15 Have you ever...?

1 I've only ever been sailing once, and that was on my ninth birthday, when my brother took his girlfriend out in her boat very late at night – it must have been eleven or twelve – and I was allowed out specially because it was my birthday. And I was allowed to take a fishing line with me and trail it over the side and I actually caught a fish.

2 No, I haven't acted in a play, but I was in an opera. I was one of the people on stage who had to do things. Not sing, because I can't sing that well but I just had to be there and do things. But it was good fun – I really enjoyed it.

3 Yes, I have. When I was 16 my brother had a motorbike and I wanted to have a go on it. And he put me on and started me off, but unfortunately he didn't tell me how to stop, and I went round this square about four times, and each time he shouted out to me. And in the end he managed to tell me. But I was quite frightened.

4 Yes, last week in fact. We went to see Hamlet at the Old Vic, and it was marvellous.

5 No, I haven't. I think to go into a casino you need lots of money, and you need to have a streak in your that wants to lose that money or win it or whatever it is that makes you want to go into a casino, I don't have it.

Unit 16 Rock climbing

A Once I had tried rock climbing, I decided that I really liked it myself quite a lot, because it wasn't a strenuous sport, it wasn't an endurance sport, not like walking in the hills – that you just have to keep plodding on – but rock climbing was fast and exciting, and funnily enough it's not so much like a sport, it's more like problem solving – that I think is the interesting thing. And even something which is small, a little boulder that's maybe 12 feet high, and doesn't look in any way unusual or difficult, can still present you with a lot of problems, and you can get very absorbed in trying to make your, find a way to make yourself move up instead of just over or stay still, and so in that sense it's an unusual sport, I think.

B What's been the most exciting thing that's happened to you in rock climbing?

A The most scary incident was actually coming off a rock in a place in Italy where I was climbing, and it wasn't terribly steep, so instead of falling free on the rope and being stopped, which happens so fast that you are really hardly aware of – you don't have time to be frightened. In this case, because it was a more sloping mountainside, I actually was bouncing and slithering all the way down, and I kept thinking 'I'm going to hurt myself, I'm definitely going to hurt myself, if I hit another time I'm going to hurt myself, I'm going break my arm, I'm going to break my leg,' and I had plenty of time to have all these bad thoughts, and be very scared indeed, and think 'Oh suppose the rope breaks or doesn't hold.'

Unit 17 Radio phone-in

A And we have Susan on the phone, who's phoning us from Woking. Susan, can you hear?

B Yes, I can. Hello.

A Hello. Um, Susan, what's your problem?

B Well, you see the thing is, I have a very good relationship with my husband, we've been married about five years now, but a few months ago he got a new job. And he works very hard, and when he comes home in the evening he's exhausted, and all he wants to do is sit in front of the telly and go to sleep. (*I see.*) Well, I work too, but what I want to do in the evenings is go out and have some fun and relax a bit, and you know he won't come with me, he really won't, and – I just don't know what to do.

A Chris, have you got any ideas how we can help Susan?

C Yes. Susan, I would suggest you actually talk to him about the problem. Talk to him – see if you can get him to come out with you shall we say for a couple of nights in the week, and then you perhaps stay at home watching the telly for the other couple of ... compromise, that's the thing – work at it and compromise.

D Um, Susan, if I can come in here. What I would suggest is – I don't know if you've tried this, but maybe you arrange to go out with some friends on your own, you know, some girlfriends or something, to the cinema, say. If he wants to stay at home, that's fine, but I don't think you should let him stop you from doing what you want.

A There you are, Susan – I hope that's helped you, and from all of us here we very much hope that you sort things out quickly. OK, we're moving on now to Sharon, who's calling us from...

Unit 18 A security guard

1 A Can you tell me what sort of work do you do?

B Yes, I'm a Securicor guard.

A I see. What does that involve?

B Well, er Securicor guards are hired by companies to guard their buildings during the day and sometimes during the night, and that's precisely what we do. Our job is to prevent people from breaking into these buildings , and to look after all aspects of security, really.

2 A What particular aspects about the job do you enjoy?

B Um, well it's, there's a certain amount of variety, you don't always work in the same place, so you travel a little bit. The people are very friendly, um..

A Anything you don't like about it?

B Oh, quite a lot, yes. The pay's not very good, it can be very boring, and you have to work very long hours.

A So you don't get much free time?

B That's right. Not if you want to earn overtime, which is really how you earn a decent wage.

A And what would be a decent wage?

B Well, in order to earn say £150 a week you have to work, ooh a good 70, 80 hours a week.

A It's a long week.

B It is, yes, yes.

Unit 19 Two stories

A I had a very embarrassing experience recently. I went to a friend's wedding, and it all went very successfully, and they had a video made of the wedding and the party – the reception afterwards. And a few weeks later they invited us round to go and watch the video, because it had, it had just arrived. So we went round, and there we were watching the video of the wedding and the reception, and at one point we suddenly noticed the father of the groom stealing the wallet out of a coat in a cloakroom, and it was very clear to see so it was extremely embarrassing, and I didn't know what to do or say really. In the end, I just had to pretend that I hadn't seen anything.

B This happened to me a few years ago now on the Underground in London. And it was a Saturday and I was going to do some shopping, and the carriage that I was in was full of football supporters. They were all quite young, I mean they weren't, they weren't men, they were boys, they were I would think 13, 14, something like that. And first of all there was just a lot of noise, and then they started rocking the carriage of the train. And it was absolutely terrifying. The train was very full by this time and I don't like crowded places anyway, but the rocking and the noise were really very very frightening indeed. And eventually the doors of the train opened, and I got out – I could hardly stand up – and got onto the platform and just collapsed in tears on a seat. It was awful – even now thinking about it I get quite shaky and frightened – it was horrible.

Unit 20 Famous people

1 This person usually wore black. She er, I remember that – her always as being old, but she was only old because she lived to a very old age. When she was young she was very pretty, but the picture we have of her, I think, is of somebody very old, dressed all in black, with a sort of – the hair tied in a tight bun, and she didn't often laugh.

2 He was a short man, who had been very elegant and always wore a uniform which was white trousers, tight white trousers and a short blue jacket with gold embroidery. He also wore boots, he had dark hair, and dark eyes. His nose was pointed, and he had a small mouth and quite a pointed chin, which made him look as though he was listening all the time. He also wore a hat, usually, a three-pointed hat.

3 She was quite a tall woman and she had a very striking face, quite an angular face. She was dark-skinned, and she had greying hair – it became more grey as the time went by. A very peaceful looking person, and a very impressive looking woman. Very striking indeed, and in fact I think as she got older she became more striking.

Unit 21 Driving test

Well, you come out of the main driving test centre and your instructor will ask you where your car is, and to take him to your car. So you walk up to it, get in, put your safety belt on, and the instructor gets in the other side. And he normally has a clipboard with various bits of paper and he starts to make little ticks and crosses even as early on in the test as that, and you're thinking to yourself 'Have I done something wrong already?' Then he'll ask you to drive, drive off. You'll drive along the road, then the instructor will ask you to turn left or right, ask you what motoring sign you've just passed and you have to tell him, then he'll ask you to do perhaps an emergency stop, pretending that a child has run into the road and you must put your foot down on the brake really quickly, and then drive on. He'll be looking to see that you're confident in the car. You find out if you've passed at the end of perhaps an hour-long test. He'll ask you to drive back into the car park at the, of the test centre, and you'll stop and think 'What is he going to say? Have I passed or failed?' And he takes out a bit of paper, and if it's pink you've failed, if it's green you've passed.

Unit 22 Living in a hot climate

I think the hottest place I've ever lived in is Kuwait, in the Arabian Gulf. It's certainly very hot most of the year, but particularly in July and August of course – it can reach up to 53 degrees centigrade in, in late July. It's a dry heat rather than a humid one though, so you're not as hot as you would be say in England perhaps if it reached 50 degrees. And of course everything is air-conditioned, so you're hardly ever out in it when it's as hot as that. The cars are air-conditioned, the schools are air-conditioned, every office is air-conditioned, your houses are air-conditioned, so you just basically just drive to a place with your a/c on in the car, leap out, run into your school or your office, stay there all day, usually having to put a jacket on 'cause it's often really quite cool inside, then you jump back into your car again and drive home. Uh, the water's often too hot to swim in, the sea water that is, during the summer. It's usually too hot even to sunbathe in the middle of summer – you just feel that your skin is sizzling.

Unit 23 24 hours

A Mary, er last Friday. Do you remember how much time you spent working?

B Well, I was spring cleaning at home actually, and it just seems to go on and on. I suppose about six hours actually.

A Um and what about travel?

B Well, travel's funny I suppose going to the shops, does that count? I, I do that quite often, I sometimes go twice or maybe three times a day. The shops are just at the top of the road. So, I suppose I spend about, mm a couple of hours travelling.

A Um, meals, what about eating?

B Eating, hmm, don't get much chance for that really. I have a little boy, you know, and er eating's very er haphazard. I suppose I spend two quarter of an hours, lunchtime and teatime, and then I have an evening meal. Sometimes the evening meal's a bit more leisurely. I suppose about an hour and a half really.

A How much time do you think you spent talking to people on Friday?

B Well, as I say it's really just going to the shops. I, I talk to the shopkeepers a lot. Oh, I suppose an hour, an hour talking.

A What about reading?

B Oh, well I don't get much chance to read myself, but I read to my little boy a lot. Um, that can be about three hours a day.

A Do you watch TV at all?

B Well, I like to, but of course I, I fall asleep at the end of the day. There are certain programmes I like to watch. I'd say about two hours.

A And finally, what about sleep?

B Huh, I like sleep. Oh, about five hours a night. Quite often it's broken sleep.

Unit 24 Choosing a painting

I'd certainly choose this one here with the landscape, with the sea in the background. I find that one particularly attractive. It's a very warm painting, I think. And I'd also take the portrait of the young girl, the darker one, which is a very peaceful painting, I think. I'm not so sure about the other portrait, the – with very bright colours. I would find that perhaps rather disturbing to have on a wall. The street scene, I don't know – it's interesting for a few moments but perhaps not for a long time. The strange figure with the red heart, I think, yes I think I'd like that one but maybe not in a room, perhaps in a hall for looking at as I walked past it, maybe. And the abstract painting with the shapes, I don't think I'd have that one, no, I think I'd grow bored with that one rather quickly.

The one I like best is the head and shoulders of the young woman. She's such a peaceful looking person, I think. And although the colours are not very startling, they're very gentle, and I feel really that it's a very relaxing picture to look at.

Answer key

Unit 13 Comparison

A Comparative and superlative

smaller; smallest
fatter; fattest
wider; widest
heavier; heaviest
more careful; most careful
more exciting; most exciting
more intelligent; most intelligent
better; best
worse; worst
farther; farthest (*or* further; furthest)
more; most

B Opposites

1 Silver is *cheaper* than gold.
2 Sheep are *older* than lambs.
3 Aluminium is *lighter* than steel.
4 Arizona is *drier* than California.
5 Reading is *easier* than listening.
6 The West is *richer* than the Third World.
7 Mars is *colder* than Venus.

C World records

1 The USSR is the largest country in the world.
2 The whale is the largest mammal (animal) in the world.
3 The cheetah is the fastest animal (mammal) in the world.
4 The Nile is the longest river in the world.
5 M. Everest is the highest mountain in the world.
6 The Sahara is the sunniest place in the world.
7 Beluga is the best (most expensive) caviare in the world.

Listening: The most and the least

1 *a* A   *b* B   *c* B   *d* A   *e* A   *f* B
2 *a* None of them
  b Switzerland: B and C
     Mexico: B
     Japan: None of them
  c Switzerland: A
     Mexico: A
     Japan: C

Pronunciation: Reduced vowels (3)

2 *a* 1 He doesn't speak to me any more.
  b 2 Careful! Those dogs are dangerous.
  c 1 Was the exam difficult?
  d 2 Where do you work?
  e 2 What does that word mean?
  f 2 You can sit wherever you like?
  g 1 Does she play chess? I think she does.
  h 2 His grandparents were Italian.
  i 2 I was there a few days ago.
  j 2 Are the children in bed?
  k 1 There weren't any seats left.
  l 2 How was the film? It was very good.

Dictation

1 London is Britain's largest city. Its most famous buildings are Buckingham Palace and the Houses of Parliament.
2 The greatest English writer, William Shakespeare, was born in Stratford-on-Avon in 1564. His most famous play is probably *Hamlet*.
3 The wettest place in Britain is the Lake District. It has about 440 cm (centimetres) of rain a year.
4 The River Severn is the longest river in Britain. It is 354 km (kilometres) long.

Reading: Four planets

1 T (It's 147 years)   7 F (Only 10 times bigger)
2 T   8 F (Pluto is)
3 T   9 T (Venus's is much thicker)
4 F (Venus is hotter)   10 T
5 T   11 T (It's the brightest)
6 T (Pluto's the lightest)

Unit 14 About town

A Guests

Possible answers:
1 take him to a nightclub; go to a casino
2 go sightseeing with her; take her to sit in the park; take her to a museum or an exhibition
3 take them to a football match; go to a sports centre; go swimming; take them to the cinema; take them to the zoo
4 go shopping with them; go sightseeing; go to a place with good views of the town; go to a nightclub or a disco(thèque)

B Giving directions

Possible answers:
1 Go under that bridge and then go straight on across the river, past the park, and turn left at the end of the road. You'll see the university on the left.

2 Yes. Go straight on down this road, and turn right at the church. The swimming pool's down there on the left.

3 – Excuse me, how do I get to the station?
– Take the first turning on the left, and then turn right at the supermarket. The station's at the end of the road.

C Describing towns

Possible answers:
1 There's a university, there are lots of cheap cafés and there's a good bookshop.
2 It's got some beautiful old buildings and it's by the sea.
3 There's nothing to do in the evenings, it's very small and it hasn't got a theatre.
4 There are lots of parks, it's got good schools, and there isn't too much traffic.

Listening: Living in London

1 *a* W; bad   *c* W; bad   *e* M; good
  b M; good   *d* W; bad   *f* M; good
2 *Possible answers:*
  b The theatre's 15 minutes from my home.
  c Aeroplanes go over every two minutes.
  d People are extremely rude.
  e You can buy fresh croissants.
  f It's very cosmopolitan.

Sound and spelling: Words with *y*

2 B dry   B typist
  A carry   A hungry
  A friendly   B trying
3 *a* married *c* easier *e* parties
  b cries   *d* enjoyed *f* stays
4 Why are you typing so slowly?
  It's the friendliest city in the world.
  I'm trying to dry my hair.
  He gets angry very easily.

Dictation

Drive down Sunset Boulevard, probably the most famous street in Los Angeles. Here you can see every side of the city's character – cheap nightclubs side by side with smart boutiques and expensive restaurants. At the western end of the Boulevard is the Beverly Hills Hotel, where visiting film stars, directors and writers go to sign their contracts.

Writing skills: Reason and contrast

2 *a* Although *b* As/Because *c* but; so
  d so; but
3 *Possible answers:*
  a As it's a small town, it's easy to get to know people, and people are very friendly.
  b As there are factories all round the town the air's very polluted, so it's a very unhealthy place to live.
  c Although it's a large industrial town and it's quite

ugly, I like living there because it has a friendly atmosphere.
d Although it's only a small town, it's very lively and there's lots to do in the evenings, and as it's by the sea it's very popular with tourists.

Unit 15 Past and present

A Irregular squares

Top left: 1 ▶ left 1 ▼ lost 2 found 3 swum
Top right: 1 slept 2 flown 3 won 4 spent
Bottom left: 1 bought 2 sold 3 done 4 gone
Bottom right: 1 written 2 grown 3 woken
  4 taken 5 been

B Not … yet

1 She hasn't found a flat yet.
2 They haven't come back yet.
3 He hasn't got up yet.
4 We haven't given up (smoking) yet.
5 The bus hasn't arrived yet.
6 I haven't left university yet.

D Questions of experience

Possible questions:
2 Have you ever driven a car?
3 Have you ever swallowed a fishbone?
4 Have you ever been to the Caribbean?
5 Have you ever spoken French in France?
6 Have you ever eaten Beluga caviare?
7 Have you ever acted in a play?
8 Have you ever been water skiing?

Listening: Have you ever …?

1 1 … been sailing?   4 … seen a play by
  2 … acted in a play?   Shakespeare?
  3 … ridden a motorbike?   5 … been to a casino?
2 1 has been sailing; on his ninth birthday; yes
  2 has acted in an opera; don't know; yes
  3 has ridden a motorbike; when she was 16; no
  4 has seen *Hamlet*; last week; yes
  5 hasn't been to a casino
3 *a* 3 – She went round the square four times.
  b 1 – He went sailing on his ninth birthday.
  c 2 – She was one of the people on stage.
  d 5 – You need lots of money to go into a casino.
  e 4 – She saw *Hamlet* at the Old Vic.

Pronunciation: Falling intonation

2 *a* I live in London.
  b We need more petrol.
  c Give it to me.
  d The matches are in the cupboard.
  e What are they doing?
  f We've just bought a new house.
  g They're watching television.

Dictation

Police are searching for four children who have been missing from their home near Glasgow for nearly 24 hours. The three five-year-old girls and a boy of three were last seen early yesterday afternoon by a neighbour. No-one has seen them since. Police have organised a search of the neighbourhood to try to find the four children.

Reading: Varieties of English

1 *a* 3   *b* 4   *c* 2   *d* 5   *e* 1   *f* 6
2 *a* No – he's still painting it (*text 3*)
  b No, it isn't (*text 5*)
  c Yes – he's leaving her (*text 6*)
  d Five – *Wildfire* and four others (*text 4*)
  e Teacher of business English (*text 2*)
  f David; yes (*text 1*)

Unit 16 Towns

A Two kinds of activity

1 guitar	7 jogging
2 knit	8 jump
3 dancing	9 football
4 cooking	10 riding
5 collects	11 golf
6 poetry	12 motor
	13 garden

A indoor   B outdoor

B Go, play and do

1 play; do	4 going; playing; went
2 do; goes	5 did; went; played
3 playing; played	

Listening: Rock climbing

1 *a* ✔	*d* ✗
b ✗	*e* ✔
c ✔	*f* ✔

2 b
3 *Possible answer:*
  'Help! I'm going to break my arm.'
  'I'm definitely going to hurt myself.'

Sound and spelling: Words with *r*

2 D flower	E during
B hear	B we're
A they're	C fire
E cure	A where
D hour	B near
A hair	C drier

3 Where's our hair drier?
  They're sitting near the fire.
  We're sending them some flowers to cheer them up.
  There's a shower upstairs in the bathroom.

Dictation

I'm very interested in languages, because when I go abroad I like to speak with the people there. I try to play the guitar – I don't play very well but every week I meet a friend and we both enjoy ourselves playing together. I live very near the sea. All through the year I go for walks along the shore, and in the summer I go swimming every day.

Writing skills: Sequence (2)

2 *a* I first met him at a party in London. About a year later I saw him again.
  b She put the phone down. After a few seconds, she picked it up again and dialled a number.
3 *Possible answers:*
  a and; A few minutes later; and
  b and; After half an hour
  c First; then; and; About an hour later
4 *Possible answer:*
  Monica knew exactly what to do. She wrote a letter and put it on the table. The letter said 'Goodbye, Edward. I've had enough.' Then she packed a small suitcase and called a taxi. After about ten minutes the taxi arrived. Monica closed the door and posted her keys through the letter box. Two hours later Edward arrived home.

Unit 17 Obligation

A Obligation structures

1 have to; can	5 don't have to; don't
2 mustn't	have to; can
3 must/have to; mustn't	6 Can; can; mustn't
4 must/have to	

B Childish questions

Possible answers:
1 Do I have to go to the dentist's?
2 Can I have chips for lunch?
3 Do you have to go home now?
4 Can we stay up for a bit?
5 Do I have to go to school?

C Flying rules

Possible answers:
You mustn't smoke during take-off and landing, but you can smoke at other times. You can't smoke in the non-smoking seats or in the toilet.
You can take one piece of hand baggage. You have to put it under your seat or in the overhead lockers.
When the seat belt sign is lit, you have to stay in your seat. At other times, you can walk around the plane.
You don't have to take food and drink with you. They usually give you a meal during the flight.

D Giving advice

Possible answers:

2 … you should take exercise and you shouldn't eat too much fatty food. You should eat a lot of fish, too.

3 … you ought to wear a seat belt, and you ought not to drink any alcohol. You should also obey speed limits.

4 … you should work hard, and you should pay your staff well. And you ought to be polite to your customers.

Listening: Radio phone-in

1 *a* who ~~has a job~~ is a student
 b a ~~bad~~ good relationship
 c he likes to ~~go to parties~~ stay at home
 d she prefers to ~~stay at home and read~~ go out
 e he won't ~~stay~~ go out with her

2 *a* 1 *e* 2
 b – *f* –
 c 2 *g* –
 d 1

Pronunciation: Rising intonation

2 *a* Hello. ↘ *e* Do you drink coffee? ↗
 b Hello? ↗ *f* Where are you going? ↘
 c Are you busy? ↗ *g* He's a friend of mine. ↘
 d My name's Peter. ↘ *h* He's a friend of yours? ↗

Dictation

Last year, my girlfriend wanted to take a business course but she didn't have enough money. Now she's finished the course, and has found a good job, but she hasn't offered to pay me back. I've mentioned it once or twice, but she just laughs and talks about something else. I love my girlfriend, but I want my money back too.

Unit 18 A day's work

A Types of work

1 police	law
2 secretary	phone
3 actor	plays
4 nurse	patients
5 receptionist	deal
6 manager	money
7 porter	carry
8 writer	books
9 decorator	houses
10 student	read
11 assistant	customers
12 occupations	What do you do?

B Careers

1 applied; get
2 work; started (got); enjoying; leave
3 get
4 lost; looking (applying)
5 working
6 started; was; retires (leaves); get

Listening: A security guard

1 Securicor guards are hired by companies.
 Their job is to guard buildings.
 They prevent people from breaking into them.

2 *a* Yes *d* No *g* No
 b Yes *e* Yes
 c No *f* Yes

Sound and spelling: Hard and soft *c* and *g*

2 S ceiling H figure
 S orange H secret
 H copy S agent
 H capital S piece
 S fence H apricot
 H magazine S fridge

3 I think orange is an ugly colour.
 That magazine costs fifty cents a copy.
 The capital city is full of secret agents.
 There's a large dog behind the garden fence.

Dictation

1 I work in a hotel. I sit at the desk by the entrance. I deal with enquiries and reservations. Guests leave their keys with me when they go out.

2 I work for a large company. I have my own office and a secretary. I look after the company's money. Once a year I calculate the company's profits. It's a very well paid job.

Writing skills: Letter writing

2 *a* Elizabeth Burke
 b Don
 c Douglas Trafford
 d Miranda

Revision and extension Units 13–18

1 Sentences

1 don't have to
2 easiest language
3 more expensive than *or* dearer than
4 haven't found it
5 shouldn't eat *or* ought not to eat
6 've never *or* haven't
7 you mustn't

2 Asking questions

1 Who's taller, John or Richard?
2 Do I have to wear a suit?
3 Can/Could you tell me the way to the nearest bank?
4 Do you like/enjoy skiing ?
5 Have you ever played tennis?
6 Have they woken up yet? or Are they awake yet?
7 Are you still working for *Argos Travel*?

3 Prepositions

1 to a jazz concert
2 from her old job; for a new one
3 for my keys
4 at university
5 at the traffic lights; at the end; of the road
6 out of the window
7 into the net
8 for a package tour company; after the tourists; with any problems

4 Word order

1 They don't go to the theatre any more.
2 What time do you have to get to work?
3 She doesn't enjoy working as a tourist guide.
4 Go straight down this road and turn right.
5 Doctors earn more money than nurses.
6 I think Prague is the most beautiful city in Europe.
or Prague is the most beautiful city in Europe, I think.

Unit 19 Narration

A What were they doing?

Possible answers:

2 … were watching TV.	6 … was getting dressed.
3 … was having a bath.	7 … was having a shave.
4 … was writing a letter.	8 … was doing the ironing.
5 … were cooking dinner.	9 … was playing cards.

B Short stories

Two possible answers:
1 My brother was practising the piano yesterday when he smelled smoke. He looked down and saw his cigarette lying on the carpet, so he picked it up quickly.
2 I was painting my bedroom ceiling the other day when I lost my balance and fell off the ladder. Luckily, I landed on the bed, so I wasn't hurt.

C … -ing … -ing …

2 … coming out of a hotel, carrying two suitcases.
3 … sitting by the road, playing the saxophone.
4 … wearing a helmet, digging a hole in the road.
5 … standing by a piano, singing.
6 … standing by a car, looking at the engine.
7 … sitting in a café, drinking coffee.

Listening: Two stories

1 Story A: embarrassing, groom, reception, video, wallet
Story B: carriage, frightened, noise, platform, supporters, terrifying, underground
2 Story A: … wedding … video … reception … invited … father … groom … wallet … embarrassing.
Story B: … an underground train … football supporters
… noise … carriage … frightened … doors … tears

Pronunciation: Intonation: questions

2 *a* – Can you ski? ↗
– Yes I can. ↘
b – My car's broken down. ↘
– Oh, has it really? ↗
c – My name's Mifanwy. ↘
– Pardon? ↗
d – Did you see the film last night? ↗
– Yes, I did. ↘
– What did you think of it? ↘

Dictation

An old man with grey hair was sitting at the piano, playing a dance tune. In the centre of the room, in a space between the tables, a man and a woman were dancing cheek to cheek. There was a young couple holding hands in the corner, talking together in low voices. At another table, a group of six men were playing cards.

Reading: Bad luck

Superstition:

1 H	2 C or I	3 I or C	4 E	5 B
6 G	7 A	8 F	9 D	

The Thief:

1 C	2 G	3 F	4 H	5 B
6 D	7 A	8 E		

Unit 20 People

A Physical appearance

Possible answers:
She was in her 20s. She was quite tall and she had short fair hair. She was wearing a green dress and sunglasses. He was a bald man in his 70s, with a short grey beard and striking blue eyes. He was carrying a walking stick.

B Character adjectives

1 friendly	5 self-confident	9 lazy
2 mean	6 hard-working	10 generous
3 bad-tempered	7 honest	11 modest
4 shy	8 easy-going	12 selfish

Listening: Famous people

a	Gandhi	g	Gandhi
b	Victoria	h	Gandhi
c	Napoleon	i	Victoria
d	Victoria	j	Gandhi
e	Napoleon	k	Napoleon
f	Victoria	l	Napoleon

Sound and spelling: Long and short vowels

2
L	mute	S	glutton
L	coping	L	scraper
S	scram	S	flitted
L	pane	L	inducing
L	strive	S	spottiest
S	petty	L	refinery

3 They're having dinner in the dining room.
He likes telling jokes.
She's writing a letter to the newspaper.
Are they winning the game or losing?

Dictation

1 It's a little stone cottage, it's grey stone, and it's very small, and there's some smoke coming out of the chimney.
2 Well, it needs a lot of work. Everything's neglected and overgrown. Very tall flowers, and very long grass.
3 It's a huge kind of lake, and the water's dark and calm, and there are fish in it. It's cold to swim in, but good too.

Writing skills: Relative clauses (1)

2 a I live in Stenton, which is a small village near Cambridge.
b I've got three sisters, who are all older than me.
c I've got a younger brother, who's in the army.
d Pandas, which only eat bamboo, are becoming very rare.
3 a which was built in 70s
b who are also staying in Paris
c which is a kind of sausage
d which is about 200 km south of here
e who's studying art here
f which still isn't very good

Unit 21 Prediction

B Questions with 'will'

1 What time (When …) will the train arrive?
2 Will it be windy tomorrow?
3 Will there be a general election this year?
4 Where will you be?
5 When will I see you again?
6 Will they lend us the money?
7 How much will the ticket cost me?

C If & unless

Possible answers:
1 If you wear a raincoat you won't get wet.
2 If you leave before dark, you'll get home safely.
3 Unless you apologise, I'll never speak to you again.
4 Unless you phone your parents, they'll worry about you.
5 Unless you go to bed early, you'll be tired tomorrow.
6 If you forget his birthday, he'll be very upset.
7 Unless you have a holiday, you'll be ill.

D Predictions with 'going to'

Possible answers:
1 It's going to rain.
2 She's going to have a baby.
3 I think I'm going to sneeze.
4 I think I'm going to be ill/sick.
5 It's going to crash (into the mountains).
6 You're going to fail. (*or* You're not going to pass.)
7 He's going to win (the race).
8 He's going to be all right.

Listening: Driving test

1 1 Which is your car?
2 OK, off you go.
3 Turn right at the crossroads.
4 What did that road sign say?
5 Stop!
6 Park the car just here.
7 Well, I'm glad to say you've passed your test.
2 a At a driving test centre.
b Put you seat belt (safety belt) on.
c A clipboard and some papers.
d It means you've failed the test.

Pronunciation: Contrastive stress

2 a She was a **maths** teacher.
b She **was** a maths teacher.
c My **moth**er usually gets up early.
d My mother **us**ually gets up early.
e I didn't see him **yes**terday.
f I didn't **see** him yesterday.

Dictation

1 Before you give blood they need to find out which blood group you belong to. So the nurse will take a small sample of blood from the end of your finger.
2 Just lie down and relax. The nurse will attach a needle to your arm, and the blood will flow down into a bag beside your bed. You don't have to do anything at all.

Reading: Star gazing

1
a	Sagittarius	f	Taurus and Pisces
b	Pisces	g	Taurus
c	Sagittarius and Libra	h	Libra and Taurus
d	Taurus	i	Pisces and Taurus
e	Libra and Sagittarius	j	Pisces

Unit 22 Around the world

A On the map

1 lake	5 border	9 desert
2 continent	6 forest	10 island
3 volcano	7 ocean	11 coast
4 river	8 mountain	12 environment

C International quiz

1 *a* Scotland   *d* Hungary
  b Thailand   *e* Ireland (Republic of)
  c Turkey   *f* Austria

2 *a* Brazilian   *d* South African
  b Portuguese   *e* Polish (a Pole)
  c Canadian   *f* Danish (a Dane)

3 *a* Japanese   *d* Finnish
  b Italian   *e* Russian
  c French

4 *a* Spanish   *d* Arabic
  b Dutch   *e* Greek
  c German   *f* Chinese

Listening: Living in a hot climate

1 Yes	6 Yes
2 July and August	7 No (they're air-conditioned)
3 – (doesn't say)	8 Yes (in air-conditioned
4 No	buildings)
5 – (doesn't say)	9 No (Not in summer)

Sound and spelling: Words with *s*

2 /s/ press   /z/ buys
  /z/ busy   /s/ scream
  /s/ coughs   /z/ climbs
  /s/ messy   /s/ listen
  /z/ princes   /z/ please
  /s/ princess   /z/ trousers
3 impress   essential
  disease   confused
  discloses   assumes
  distances   blossom

Dictation

The climate of Egypt is mainly hot and dry. Apart from the Valley of the River Nile, which runs through the country from south to north, it consists entirely of desert. In the summer, the temperature often reaches 45° in the south of the country, and 30° in the north. In winter, the weather is cooler, and along the north coast it is often cloudy, with occasional rain.

Writing skills: Relative clauses (2)

1 *a* Jakarta, which is the capital of Indonesia, has...
  b The Cape Verde Islands, which used to be a Portuguese colony, have been ...
  c ... of Charles I, who was King of England from 1600 to 1649
  d In Alaska, where the temperature often falls below −30°, it can be ... *or* In Alaska it can be dangerous to go out in winter, when the temperature ...

2 *Possible answer:*
  If you have time, you should visit the Parrot Café, which is in a small side street behind the harbour. It's the oldest café in the town and it's very popular with fishermen, who sit there all day playing cards. The owner, who is in his 80s, is a retired sea captain. Next to the Parrot Café there's a small museum, where you can see treasure from an old sailing ship, which sank near the town in the 17th century.

Unit 23 Duration

A For or since?

1 for; since	4 for; since; for
2 for; for	5 since; for
3 for; since	6 since; for; since; since

B Talking about duration

1 I've known him since my birthday party.
2 She's been asleep for a long time.
3 They've been learning Arabic since last autumn.
4 We've been divorced for six months.
5 I've been reading this book since yesterday lunchtime.
6 She's had her guitar since Christmas.
  (*or* She's been playing the guitar since Christmas.)
7 He's been wearing glasses for five years.

C How long ...?

1 How long have you known her?
2 How long have you had it?
3 How long have they been (staying) here?
4 How long has he been playing (the piano)?
5 How long has she been learning (speaking) it?
6 How long have you had it?
7 How long has she been there?

Listening: 24 hours

1 *a* 6 hours   *e* 3 hours
  b 2 hours   *f* 2 hours
  c 1½ hours   *i* 5 hours
  d 1 hour
2 *a* Housewife   *d* Evening meal
  b One   *e* Children's books
  c No   *f* Very tired

Pronunciation: Dialogues

A – I'm going to Spain next week.
  – Are you? Who are you going with?
  – Mary.
  – Who?

B – Would you like to come to the cinema tonight?
  – No, I'm afraid I can't. I'm busy tonight.
  – Are you free tomorrow, then?
  – No, I'm busy tomorrow, too.

C – Have you ever been to Malaysia?
  – No I haven't, but I've been to Thailand.
  – Oh. Were you there on holiday?
  – No, not on holiday. It was a business trip.

Dictation

1 I go to lectures from 9 till 12, and I have classes from 2 to 4. Apart from that I spend about 3 hours in the library or working in my room.
2 My flat's near the university. I don't spend more than half an hour a day travelling.
3 I don't eat breakfast, and I only have time for a quick lunch. Dinner's more relaxed. I suppose I spend about 2 hours altogether having meals.

Unit 24 But is it art?

A Places and people

play: theatre; playwright; actor; producer
opera: opera house; composer; orchestra/conductor; singer
symphony: concert hall; composer; orchestra; conductor
film: cinema; director; producer; actor
painting: art gallery; painter; exhibition

Listening: Choosing a painting

2 A ? Interesting for a few moments.
  B ? I'd find it rather disturbing.
  C ✗ I'd grow bored with it rather quickly.
  D ✔ It's a very warm painting.
  E ✔ A very peaceful painting.
  F ✔ Suitable for a hall.
3 E

Sound and spelling: Words with *th*

2 /θ/ earth   /θ/ thumb
  /ð/ theirs   /θ/ mouth
  /ð/ brother   /ð/ these
  /θ/ months   /ð/ neither
  /ð/ northern   /ð/ breathe
  /ð/ leather   /θ/ cloth
  /θ/ both   /ð/ clothes

3 I *think the* ship's sinking.
  Look – *there's another* mouse.
  Is the *clothes* shop open?
  Are *both those* seats taken?
  I taught for *three* years at a secondary school.
  Congratulations on the *birth* of your daughter.

Dictation

He reached the bed, took off his clothes and slid under the covers. He heard the soft breaths of the stranger and knew that he would never be able to get to sleep.

'By the way,' he said hesitantly, after a while. 'My name is Schwamm.'

'Uh-huh,' said the stranger.

'Yes.'

'Did you come here for a conference?'

'No, and you?'

'No.'

'On business?' asked Schwamm.

'Not really.'

'I've probably got the most remarkable reason a man could have for travelling to this city,' said Schwamm.

Writing skills: Sequence (3)

2 *a* A few weeks after he bought...
    or A few weeks after buying...
  b Two years later, she had...
  c Before leaving the house...
    or Before I left the house...
  d Two years after joining...
    or Two years after he joined...
  e While staying in India, she...
3 *Possible answer:*
After she said goodbye to her friends, she went back to the hotel. Fortunately, there was no one at the desk, so she quickly took the key for Room 24 and took the lift to the second floor. Before opening the door she put her ear to the keyhole and listened carefully. Then she slipped quietly into the room and switched the light on. A few minutes later, she found what she was looking for. The book was in the wardrobe under some shirts. She looked quickly through it, and then, after putting the book back in the wardrobe, she left the room.

Revision and extension Units 19–24

1 Verb forms

1 spent; playing
2 was standing; came; pushed
3 's been playing; 'll win
4 leave; 'll call
5 sitting; playing; was singing
6 'm going to be

2 Asking questions

1 How much (money) will they pay (me)? or
  How much (money) will I get/earn?
2 How long have you had that jacket?
3 What does he look like?
4 What were you talking about?
5 What's the climate/weather like in Malaysia?
6 How long have you been giving/going to/taking/having private lessons?
7 What do you think of that picture?

3 Prepositions

1 along the road;
  at the bus stop
2 in her fifties
3 at the airport;
  through customs
4 on the coast;
  in the mountains
5 for nearly an hour;
  since 9 o'clock this morning
6 from 8 in the morning;
  to/till/until 6 in the evening;
  to an evening class
7 of the woman's face;
  by Picasso

4 Word order

1 The telegram arrived while they were having lunch.
  or
  While they were having lunch, the telegram arrived.
2 She's a tall woman with long dark hair.
3 How long will it take to get home?
4 Her brother is about 25 years old.
5 The best time to visit Scotland is the early summer.
  or
  The early summer is the best time to visit Scotland.
6 If you don't hurry you might not get a ticket. *or*
  You might not get a ticket if you don't hurry.

Irregular verbs

Infinitive	Simple past	Past participle
be	was/were	been
become	became	become
begin	began	begun
blow	blew	blown
break	broke	broken
bring	brought	brought
build	built	built
buy	bought	bought
can	could	(been able)
catch	caught	caught
choose	chose	chosen
come	came	come
cost	cost	cost
cut	cut	cut
do	did	done
draw	drew	drawn
dream	dreamt	dreamt
drink	drank	drunk
drive	drove	driven
eat	ate	eaten
fall	fell	fallen
feed	fed	fed
feel	felt	felt
find	found	found
fly	flew	flown
forget	forgot	forgotten
get	got	got
give	gave	given
go	went	gone (been)
have	had	had
hear	heard	heard
hide	hid	hidden
hit	hit	hit
hold	held	held
hurt	hurt	hurt
keep	kept	kept
know	knew	known
lay	laid	laid
learn	learnt	learnt
leave	left	left
lend	lent	lent
let	let	let
lie	lay	lain
lose	lost	lost
make	made	made
mean	meant	meant
meet	met	met
pay	paid	paid
put	put	put
read	read	read
ride	rode	ridden
ring	rang	rung
rise	rose	risen
run	ran	run
say	said	said
see	saw	seen
sell	sold	sold
send	sent	sent
set	set	set
shake	shook	shaken
shine	shone	shone
shoot	shot	shot

Infinitive	Simple past	Past participle
show	showed	shown
shut	shut	shut
sing	sang	sung
sit	sat	sat
sleep	slept	slept
speak	spoke	spoken
spell	spelt	spelt
spend	spent	spent
stand	stood	stood
steal	stole	stolen
swim	swam	swum
take	took	taken
teach	taught	taught
tear	tore	torn
tell	told	told
think	thought	thought
throw	threw	thrown
understand	understood	understood
wake	woke	woken
wear	wore	worn
win	won	won
write	wrote	written

Phonetic symbols

Vowels

Symbol	Example
/iː/	tree /triː/
/i/	many /ˈmeni/
/ɪ/	sit /sɪt/
/e/	bed /bed/
/æ/	back /bæk/
/ʌ/	sun /sʌn/
/ɑː/	car /kɑː/
/ɒ/	hot /hɒt/
/ɔː/	horse /hɔːs/
/ʊ/	full /fʊl/
/uː/	moon /muːn/
/ɜː/	girl /gɜːl/
/ə/	arrive /əˈraɪv/
	water /ˈwɔːtə/
/eɪ/	late /leɪt/
/aɪ/	time /taɪm/
/ɔɪ/	boy /bɔɪ/
/əʊ/	home /həʊm/
/aʊ/	out /aʊt/
/ɪə/	hear /hɪə/
/eə/	there /ðeə/
/ʊə/	pure /pjʊə/

Consonants

Symbol	Example
/p/	pull /pʊl/
/b/	bad /bæd/
/t/	take /teɪk/
/d/	dog /dɒg/
/k/	cat /kæt/
/g/	go /gəʊ/
/tʃ/	church /tʃɜːtʃ/
/dʒ/	age /eɪdʒ/
/f/	for /fɔː/
/v/	love /lʌv/
/θ/	thick /θɪk/
/ð/	this /ðɪs/
/s/	sit /sɪt/
/z/	zoo /zuː/
/ʃ/	shop /ʃɒp/
/ʒ/	leisure /ˈleʒə/
/h/	house /haʊs/
/m/	make /meɪk/
/n/	name /neɪm/
/ŋ/	bring /brɪŋ/
/l/	look /lʊk/
/r/	road /rəʊd/
/j/	young /jʌŋ/
/w/	wear /weə/

Stress

We show stress by a mark (ˈ) before the stressed syllable:
later /ˈleɪtə/; arrive /əˈraɪv/; information /ɪnfəˈmeɪʃn/